Triathlon 101

Essentials
for Multisport Success

by
John Mora

Human Kinetics

Library of Congress Cataloging-in-Publication Data

Mora, John, 1964-
    Triathlon 101 : Essentials for multisport success / by John M. Mora.
      p. cm.
    Includes bibliographical references (p.   ) and index.
    ISBN 0-88011-811-3
    1. Triathlon.   2. Triathlon--Training.   I. Title.   II. Title:
Triathlon one hundred one.   III. Title: Triathlon one hundred and
one.
    GV1060.73.M67 ·1999   98-43184
    796.42'57--dc21   CIP

ISBN: 0-88011-811-3

Acquisitions Editor: Martin Barnard; **Developmental Editor:** Elaine Mustain; **Assistant Editor:** Cassandra Mitchell; **Copyeditor:** Heather Stith; **Proofreader:** Kathy Bennett; **Indexer:** Nancy Ball; **Graphic Designer:** Nancy Rasmus; **Graphic Artist:** Yvonne Winsor; **Photo Editors:** Boyd LaFoon and Kristen King; **Cover Designer:** Jack Davis; **Photographer (cover):** Robert Oliver; **Photographer (interior):** John Mora unless otherwise noted; **Illustrators:** Line artist, John Hatton/Cartoonist, Ben Boyd/Mac artist, Tom Roberts; **Printer:** United Graphics

Human Kinetics books are available at special discounts for bulk purchase. Special editions or book excerpts can also be created to specification. For details, contact the Special Sales Manager at Human Kinetics.

Printed in the United States of America   10 9 8 7 6 5 4 3 2

Human Kinetics
Web site: http://www.humankinetics.com/

United States: Human Kinetics, P.O. Box 5076, Champaign, IL 61825-5076
1-800-747-4457

Canada: Human Kinetics, 475 Devonshire Road, Unit 100, Windsor, ON N8Y 2L5
1-800-465-7301 (in Canada only)

Europe: Human Kinetics, P.O. Box IW14, Leeds LS16 6TR, United Kingdom
+44 (0)113-278 1708

Australia: Human Kinetics, 57A Price Avenue, Lower Mitcham, South Australia 5062
(08) 82771555

New Zealand: Human Kinetics, P.O. Box 105-231, Auckland Central
09-523-3462

To Guillermo, who introduced me to marathoning.

To Jose, who introduced Guillermo and me to triathlon.

And to the Three Amigos: Guillermo, Jose, and myself—we had the best uniforms of any triathlon team. And we had one of the best times of our lives becoming triathletes.

Table of Contents ▰▰▰

Foreword

Welcome to the world of triathlon!

If you are reading this book, you're probably either a novice triathlete or aspire to become a triathlete some day soon. I congratulate you on taking the right steps to get there. You're lucky that the pioneers of the sport have learned a lot of things the hard way so that you don't have to!

I entered my first triathlon in 1984, when little information was available on triathlon training. I learned a little about triathlons back then from my college roommate, who was vastly more experienced than I was. She had finished one triathlon—one more than I had done.

Gradually over the next few years we learned the ropes through trial and error . . . how much more enjoyable cycling can be if you have padded shorts . . . how pushing too hard on the bike will make you run like your legs are made of lead pipes . . . how trying to get every grain of sand off your feet before putting on your running shoes may hurt your race time.

Now that I am an enthusiastic triathlon veteran, I often lament that our sport hasn't caught on with the masses. In this generation of fitness-consciousness, triathlon should have a broader appeal. Swimming, biking, and running as separate disciplines are always at the top of the list of the most widely participated sports. Why shouldn't the combination of the three be just as popular?

I think intimidation is a big factor. Many people associate triathlon with the much-publicized Hawaiian Ironman, a race that gives people the impression that they have to be fitness fanatics or masochists to be triathletes. The people competing in this event have trained for years to reach their level of fitness and often have invested thousands of dollars in the latest high-tech equipment. Most novices don't relish the idea of jumping in a race with the likes of these diehards. But, as this book explains, the Ironman is only the extreme end of the spectrum of triathlons and triathletes.

Even people who are aware of shorter, sprint-distance races that require a minimum of training are often intimidated to take that first step. I have met too many people that have yet to "tri" because they don't know which race to choose, what equipment they need, and what training is necessary—even though they may already be proficient in running, cycling, and swimming.

With *Triathlon 101*, John Mora fills a wide gap in triathlon training books. This easy and fun-to-read book should ease most of your fears and answer nearly all of your questions. It tells you what you need to target that race, get the proper equipment, train appropriately, and get yourself to the finish line.

There are plenty of books out there geared toward improving your times or maximizing your potential, but until now little information has been available on the fundamentals of getting into the sport of triathlon. You will see that once you are armed with that basic, but essential information, your intimidation should melt away—at least until you get to the Hawaiian Ironman!!!

Karen Smyers
Professional Triathlete
1995 Hawaiian Ironman Champion

Preface

So you want to do a triathlon—or maybe you've done one or two, but don't know the ropes quite as well as you'd like. Perhaps you're an accomplished runner, cyclist, or swimmer and want to expand your horizons. Well, get ready for an exciting sport that will challenge you in ways you never imagined. Training for multisport events is a great way to get in fantastic shape and have the time of your life.

Whether you're new to the triathlon scene or have some experience, you've probably got a few questions you want answered, such as:

- What distance triathlon should I do?
- Should I buy a wetsuit?
- What kind of bicycle do I need?
- How do I train for a triathlon?
- What should I eat the morning of a race?
- How can I learn to swim safely in open water?

You'll find answers to these questions and much, much more in *Triathlon 101*. The sole purpose of this book is to answer your important questions and provide the information you need now. Best of all, you'll find the answers you need quickly, without a lot of fancy or unnecessary information.

Triathlon isn't as simple as lacing up your running shoes and putting one foot in front of the other, but I've tried to simplify things for you by sticking to the fundamentals. What you will find here are the necessary, practical basics for a successful introduction to this exhilarating sport. This book is written for you. Everything here is for the novice triathlete and deals only with topics and information you need to safely and successfully reach your goal.

In my 10 years as a triathlon journalist, my most frequent assignments have dealt with fundamental topics such as buying your first tri-bike or open water safety tips. So I know there are a lot of beginners out there, grasping for definitive answers. No need to grasp any longer—the definitive answers are here for you in one place! Forget about the hit-or-miss advice you might get from well-meaning friends or family. This one-stop resource book has all the information you need in plain language.

Triathlon 101 is divided into three parts. Part I covers all you need to know to plan your training and racing season, including information about equipment such as wetsuits and triathlon bikes. In chapters 1 through 3, you'll learn about the sport, the jargon, how to target goals, and get set up with all the right tri gear.

The nuts and bolts of training are detailed in part II of the book. We'll tackle swimming, biking, and running in chapters 4 through 6, and then show you how to integrate all three in chapter 7. I also cover training tips to teach your body how to go from one sport to the next without missing a beat.

In part III, I cover all the things you need to know to stay on track. In chapter 8, you'll find some sports nutrition fundamentals, and you'll avoid the dreaded injury bug by reading chapter 9 before that next killer workout. Chapter 10 provides you with all the practical considerations you need to think about before that big race. Finally, chapter 11 paves the way for you to make triathlon not just a new sport for you, but a healthy, fun, and wonderfully gratifying way of life. You'll find plenty of motivation along the way. I've interviewed dozens of triathletes, both amateurs and professionals, about their early triathlon experience and included their most interesting, funny, and inspiring success stories. I've also provided checklists, tips, examples, and the resources you need to take your triathlon experience to the next level. With all these handy tools, you'll find *Triathlon 101* a practical, inspirational workbook to use on every step of your multisport adventure.

My purpose is to make triathlon more accessible and less intimidating for everyone. I think you'll find that the information on preparing, training, and racing in multisport events will make your experience less daunting and more fun.

With a growing interest in triathlon, there is a need for some basic knowledge, a step-by-step guide to the challenging prospect of competing, setting a personal best, or just plain finishing a swim-bike-run event. No matter what your reason for wanting to join the ranks of thousands of active fitness enthusiasts who embrace the growing and invigorating sport of triathlon, I hope *Triathlon 101* is just the first step toward crossing many exhilarating finish lines.

Acknowledgments

I'd like to acknowledge the following people for contributing their technical expertise to this book: Terry Laughlin, for allowing me to use materials from his Total Immersion workbook and contributing an article that was adapted for use in the swim chapter; Lauren Jensen, for her valuable tips in the cycling chapter; and Troy Jacobson, for the expertise he provided in the running chapter. For guidance on sports medicine topics, I'd like to thank: Dr. George Tsatsos, Dr. Lawrence Burns, Dr. Daryll Hobson, Dr. P. Michael Leahy, Lisa Alamar, Robert P. Nirschl, MD, and J.P. Neary, PhD.

For their input on topics regarding the sport of triathlon and equipment, thanks to: Bob Babbit, Jan Caille, Bob Langan, Dan Siever, Liz Downing, Steve Hed, Ken Souza, John Cobb, and Dan Empfield.

Many thanks to the profiled triathletes who let us peek into their unique experiences and, in the process, gave us all the gift of inspiration: Paula Newby-Fraser, Mike Greer, Butch Forsyth, Diane Berberian, Marti Hobbs, FD Moore, Joe Albert, Karl Hausmann, Mike Pigg, Melanie Mocium, and Wes Freas.

I also thank these people for their contributions in various aspects of putting the book together: Jeffrey Justice, former (and best-ever) editor of *Triathlete Magazine* (wherever you are); Shelley Berryhill, former editor of *Windy City Sports*, for assigning me all those triathlon articles; Jeff Banowitz, who continues to do the same; and Martin Barnard at Human Kinetics for his veteran editorial and triathlon guidance.

Thanks to talented cartoonist Ben Boyd for bringing his unique sense of humor to the book, and to Bob Babbit for penning most of the cartoon captions.

Also, thanks to all the cyberspace triathletes in the Usenet rec.sports.triathlon newsgroup for their input on various aspects of the book, including jargon, training schedules, and late-night inspiration. RSTers are the best!

Most of all, thanks to Margaret, for all the cuddling time we missed while I was working on the book late at night and for all your invaluable research, proofing, and editing work. Love you!

Part I
Getting Ready to Tri

Preparation is the key to your successful introduction into multisports. From knowing what distances to choose, to setting a goal, to buying the right equipment, your experience will go much smoother if you make the effort to be prepared before you start to train. The next few chapters will help you do that.

Chapter 1

So You Wanna Tri?

> "When it's good, it's really good. And when it's bad, it's still pretty good."
>
> —*Scott Tinley, comparing the Ironman Triathlon to pizza and sex*

Remember when you were a kid? Think back for a minute and remember a time that was simpler, less worrisome, and, well, more fun. Close your eyes. Think about how you used to play: chasing your friends, pedaling your first bike, going to the beach. Your friends shouting, "Let's jump in the pool! Let's go bike riding! Race you to the corner!"

See what I'm getting at? In a sense, we all grew up triathletes. Sure, we may not have swum, biked, and run in that order or traversed any significant distances, but we knew the fun of mixing things up a bit. For playful, energetic children hell-bent on having fun, running, cycling, and swimming were three very common summertime activities.

Everybody has their unique motivation for getting involved in a new activity, but I've always felt that one of the greatest lures of the multisport world is the sheer enjoyment of combining three different and challenging physical activities into one exciting sport.

The Sport for the Rest of Us

During a recent beginning triathlon seminar put on by the Chicago Triathlon Club, an interesting revelation hit me as I looked at those assembled. The attendants were no longer frustrated runners, limping to the triathlon to relieve them of their overstressed ligaments. Nor were they prune-skin swimmers, tired of following the black line at the bottom of the pool. Pedal-happy cyclists looking for a new reason to shave their legs? Nope.

Most of the attendants were true newcomers to the sport, many with little athletic background or training knowledge. They were the homemaker who never even ran a 10K, the construction worker who could barely swim one pool length, and the nurse with more dust on her Schwinn than on Leona Helmsley's tax returns. All of them were eager to become active participants in multisports, achieve fitness, and find personal satisfaction in doing triathlons.

More and more people today—no matter what their background or athletic talent—are interested in total fitness. The triathlon is the ideal sport of the new millennium for many reasons.

An Outdoor Experience

Triathlons give you the refreshing, invigorating feeling of swimming in a lake or ocean, cycling on roads that take you through striking countryside scenery, and running on a pristine trail or path. How else can you experience nature in three distinct ways, all in the span of a few hours or less? Granted, not all triathlon venues are located in national or state parks. Sometimes, as in the case of Chicago's giant Mrs. T's Triathlon, the scenery from the bike consists entirely of metal skyscrapers. Still, with the exception of indoor multisport events and big city races, the great outdoors makes the triathlon a feast for the senses and a welcome respite from urban blight.

Rural triathlons give you the opportunity to breathe in fresh air, especially important on those hills.

Variety Is the Spice of Multisport

If you've ever trained for a single sport event, such as a marathon or a long bike ride, then you know how monotonous training can get. Multisport training brings variety back to your workout routine. The simple act of not doing the same workout day in and day out will be a real lift to your body, mind, and spirit.

Tri-ing Puts the Fun Back in Fitness

For many people, fitness is drudgery. It's a daily or weekly chore, something that has to be done on a regular basis, like cleaning the house, mowing the lawn, or paying the bills. You see it all the time in health clubs—frustrated men and women who push themselves too hard for the sole purpose of burning calories or shaving those love handles. They never look like they're having fun, which is probably why most New Year's fitness resolutions don't last past the first day of spring.

Exercise doesn't have to be that way. Yes, exercise can be fun, especially when you have three sports to work with. Sure, you'll have to work hard and get your heart rate up now and then, but who says it has to be drudgery? If part of your purpose in pursuing multisports is losing weight and getting into shape, that's okay. Just try to keep it lighthearted, and you might find that you'll achieve your weight or body physique goals without feeling like you're mopping the kitchen floor.

It's a Better Balancing Act

One of the keys to success in multisport training is striking just the right balance. You'll have to become proficient at juggling types of workouts, intensity, distance, and other factors, in addition to balancing the time devoted to all three sports. To be sure, you'll need to learn from experience; trial and error are definitely part of the equation. But the skills you learn from balancing your multisport training can translate directly into the rest of your life in many positive ways.

Three's a Challenge

Although marathoning is certainly a formidable test of endurance, triathlons have now become a good alternative for the pavement-weary warrior. Triathlon training requires disciplined workouts in three different sports, and triathletes that delve into half-Ironman distance or Ironman territory must tackle significant training and possess tons of self-discipline to achieve their goal. Although you may not be setting your sights on the Hawaii Ironman Triathlon right now, completing any distance triathlon is still a formidable task.

Three's a Cinch

On the other hand, training for a short-distance triathlon is a hell of a lot easier than training for a marathon, at least in terms of total workout time. I don't mean to imply that completing your first triathlon will be a piece of cake. If you're deathly afraid of water, learning to swim may be the hardest thing you do in your life. Or if you've let yourself get out of shape, running more than a few minutes may be a big challenge. Yet a short-distance triathlon that might take you 90 minutes is certainly a more manageable goal than a 26.2-mile foot race that might take you four or five hours.

It's a Group Effort

You're not alone in your aspirations to be a totally fit triathlete. Triathlon clubs, magazines, national organizations, Web sites, and training groups are all resources that you can tap into. In particular, local clubs are a great way to learn about the sport and meet people to train with. Sure, triathlon isn't as popular in the mainstream as say running or in-line skating, but if you look hard enough, you'll probably find your ideal training partner or group.

Triathlon: Where Did It Come From?

Perhaps your exposure to triathlon came through a friend or maybe by watching the famous Ironman Triathlon in Hawaii on television. Unless you've been around triathlon for a long time, you're probably curious about the history of the sport.

The first true multisport event was a biathlon (now called duathlon, so the name doesn't conflict with the run and rifle shoot sport). Although many people have the misconception that the Hawaii Ironman was the first triathlon, the first true triathlon was a lot shorter than the grueling race you may have seen on television. The following section gives a brief rundown of the origins of the sport that you're about to jump into.

Triathlon Timeline

The sport of triathlon had its roots in duathlon, progressed to a three-sport event, and has evolved into a worldwide phenomenon.

- **1972:** San Diego lawyer David Pain, one of the founders of the masters running movement in the United States, puts on the David Pain Birthday Biathlon, consisting of a 10K run and a half-mile swim.
- **1974:** Two members of the San Diego Track Club add a bike ride to the mix and put on the first true triathlon, held on Fiesta Island near the present-day Sea World. The Mission Bay Triathlon consisted of a 2.8-mile run, a 5-mile bike ride, a .25-mile swim, a 2-mile run, and a .25-mile swim.
- **1977:** Tired of swimmers and cyclists arguing with him and his running friends about who was the better athlete, Navy commander John Collins challenges a crowd gathered at the awards party for the Oahu running relay race to go beyond a single sport. The gauntlet he threw down? Complete three separate events all in one day: the 2.4 mile Waikiki Rough Water Swim, the 115-mile Around-the-Island Bike Ride, and the 26.2-mile Honolulu Marathon. Whoever could win such a race, he announced, could call himself (no women raced the first year) an iron man.
- **1978:** After a year's preparation by John Collins, the first Ironman Triathlon is held on February 18, 1978. Fifteen men, including Collins, raced on that day. The first Ironman champion was a former Navy pentathlete, Gordon Haller.
- **1982:** Word spreads about the Ironman, courtesy of *Sports Illustrated* and ABC Sports. Millions of television viewers witness the famous 400-yard crawl of courageous triathlete Julie Moss at the finish line, putting the sport of triathlon on the media map. That same year, the United States Triathlon Series was created, bringing shorter distance races to the mainstream and paving the way for future growth.

The Sport of Triathlon Today

The preceding timeline is a short history of some events that shaped the beginnings of the triathlon. Other major events, such as the creation of the sport's United States governing body, Tri-Fed, now known as USA Triathlon, and the introduction of bicycle aero bars, have a lot to do with the sport as it is today.

Triathlete legends such as the Big Four—Dave Scott, Scott Molina, Scott Tinley, and Mark Allen—as well as female pioneers Erin Baker, Paula Newby-Fraser, Colleen Cannon, and Julie Moss, paved the way for future generations of professional triathletes. More importantly, they brought big-time media attention to a very small sport, thus bringing triathlon to people who were getting tired of running marathon after marathon.

Your Triathlon Choices

Now that you know more about triathlon's history than many tri veterans, it's a good time to talk about the variety of multisport event distances you have to choose from. Unlike some sports with very

Triathlon Facts

History shows that, although triathlon has experienced growing pains and political infighting—the kind of stuff that happens in any organized sport—multisport events are here to stay. Need proof? Here are a few facts:

Fact: Since 1980, triathlon has been one of the fastest-growing recreational sports in the United States. According to USA Triathlon, participation is growing at a steady pace, and the number of newcomers to the sport continues to increase every year.

Fact: In 1997, more than 200,000 individuals competed in at least one of 1,200 triathlons in the United States.

Fact: The opening event for the 2000 Olympics in Sydney is triathlon.

Fact: On an international level, triathlon is booming. In Australia, triathlon is taught as a sport on the high school level, and organized swim-bike-run competitions are commonplace between schools.

Fact: Over 50 percent of all triathlons are sprint distance, a very short race that requires a minimum of training. So triathlon, once perceived to be the exclusive domain of superathletes, has become a mainstream sport with options to suit every lifestyle and level of commitment.

Fact: Triathlon race directors report continued increases in participation. The Mrs. T's Triathlon in Chicago usually reports numbers in excess of 4,000 entries.

Most triathlons start on a beach, but occasionally you might enter a race that does things a little differently.

strict format guidelines, virtually any event that includes a swim, a bike ride, and a run can be called a triathlon.

There are indoor triathlons, triathlons that start with a swim and end with a swim, triathlons that have two bike legs, and mountain bike triathlons with the run and the bike held on trails, to name just a few. The triathlon is only limited by the venue and the imagination of the race director. Even though there are many unique events that deviate from the traditional, the swim-bike-run format is the most prevalent and, in all likelihood, is the kind of event that has seized your interest.

In terms of distance, again, the sky's the limit. Most triathlons, however, do fall under one of four distance categories. (But you'll probably find plenty of races that fall somewhere in between these distances, which is part of what makes triathlon unique.) The following sections describe each of the four predominant distances and provide recommendations that might help give you an idea of where you might want to set your sights.

Sprint Distance:
.75K Swim, 22K Bike Ride, and 5K Run

The trend today is toward more short-distance races. In a recent race director survey taken by USA Triathlon, over 50 percent of all triathlons were the sprint distance. In the sport's infancy, the longer distances and the "gruel-a-thon" image gave triathlon a certain degree of novelty, but nowadays the reality is that there is a greater demand for more doable events.

Case in point: The Carlsbad Triathlon, a popular California event, began to see its participation numbers decline a few years ago, from 1,000 to under 700. The race directors decided to change from the Olympic distance to a sprint distance and the numbers quickly climbed back up to over 1,000. "There are just many more people that don't have the time to train for a two-hour event, but can manage a one-hour race," says Bob Babbit, triathlon guru and publisher of *Competitor Magazine*. "Shorter events really fill up."

Sprint distance races are ideal for the following people:

- The beginning triathlete who wants to jump in and catch the multisport bug
- Hares who lose their energy in races lasting over 90 minutes
- Level-headed types that neither have the desire nor inclination to press the endurance envelope
- Time-pressed triathletes who don't have more than 5 to 10 hours a week to train for longer-distance races
- Triathletes who want to go fast the whole way

Olympic Distance:
1.5K Swim, 40K Bike Ride, 10K Run

The Olympic distance was popularized by the United States Triathlon Series, also known as the Bud Light races, during the '80s. This distance was instrumental in bringing triathlon to the mainstream. Even though it might take the average person close to three hours to complete, the Olympic distance, then called the "middle" distance, was a way to participate in a new and exciting sport without traveling to Hawaii and racing on the lava fields all day. As its name implies, this distance is also the distance triathletes from around the world race to go for the gold at the Olympics.

The Olympic distance is ideal for those who wish to push the endurance envelope beyond the two-hour boundary. If you're looking for a definite challenge and are not quite ready for a longer-course triathlon, training for an Olympic distance event can help you get into great shape.

Olympic distance races are ideal for the following people:

- Newcomers to the sport who already have a solid endurance base in an aerobic sport
- The experienced cyclist who occasionally runs
- The veteran runner who occasionally bikes
- The swimmer who plans on doing a lot more biking and running
- Triathletes who are willing to commit to 10 to 15 hours of training per week

Half-Ironman Distance:
1.2-Mile Swim, 56-Mile Bike Ride, 13.1-Mile Run

Half-Ironman races represent a serious level of competition for the triathlete looking to expand his or her endurance horizons. Whereas you might be able to eke out a sprint or maybe even an Olympic distance race on minimum training, half-Ironman distances will bite you in the butt if you haven't made a serious commitment to training long before you "toe the line" on race day.

Half-Ironman races are a hotbed of age group competition, and many of these events are Ironman qualifiers (which means you get a chance to race in Hawaii if you're fast enough). Although you may be used to seeing quite a few weekend warriors rolling in on their mountain bikes or Schwinn La Tours at sprint, or maybe even the Olympic distance races, you'd be hard-pressed to find anybody who hasn't plunked down a few grand on a sleek and super lightweight tri-machine at these events.

Don't be intimidated by this difference if you prefer the long haul and are willing to swim, bike, and run for five to six hours or more. Nobody says you can't still do it on your fat tire machine or cruiser (I've seen lot of people have a great time at these events on their old clunker). Just don't expect any bagels to be left at the finish line for you.

Half-Ironman distance races are ideal for the following people:

- Triathletes with at least one year's experience racing sprint or Olympic distance events
- Endurance cyclists with some running experience
- Runners with several half-marathons under their belts and some cycling experience
- Swimmers who plan on doing more biking and running than they'd like to think about
- Triathletes who are willing to commit to 15 to 20 hours of training per week

Ironman Distance: 2.4-Mile Swim, 112-Mile Bike Ride, 26.2-Mile Run

The Ultimate. The Big Show. The Big Hurt (or is that Frank Thomas?). What else can you say about the holy grail of triathlon? (Okay, technically, the Ironman Triathlon in Hawaii is the real holy grail of the sport, but I think anybody who does any race of this distance should be considered a Sir or Lady Galahad.) Some triathletes train

What's an Ironman Qualifier?

If you've been reading the race section of your favorite multisport magazine, or been hanging around triathlon veterans, the term "Ironman qualifier" might have popped out at you. The term refers to one of the only two ways to be allowed to race in the Ironman Triathlon in Hawaii. Because the race is so popular and only a limited number of participants are allowed for safety reasons, event officials had to find a fair way to allow only the best triathletes to race in the sweltering heat and wind of the island of Kona.

Therefore, a limited number of established races are designated every year as "Ironman qualifiers." These races are held around the world and range in length from Olympic distance up to other Ironman distance races. Participants who finish at the top of their age group in these events are awarded an Ironman slot, which allows them to enter the Big Show. Oh, and for us speed-challenged triathletes, there's still hope. A very limited number of Ironman slots (usually 50) are allocated in a lottery drawing, which anybody can get in on (for a fee).

for years to get to the point where they can traverse these distances without going into a coma.

Needless to say (but I'll say it anyway), the challenge of training and racing an Ironman distance race should not be entered into lightly. Completing an Ironman safely requires an enormous amount of preparation and commitment. Some triathletes race an entire lifetime without completing this distance, either by design or because the time commitments are too great. Training for an Ironman may also put some emotional strain on your family and interfere with your career.

Although it may seem as though I'm trying to discourage you from setting your sights on an Ironman, I am not. It is the ultimate triathlon event, and I believe the crowning achievement for any experienced triathlete who wishes to reach a landmark in his or her multisport career. The key word in that previous sentence is *experienced.* A newcomer to the sport, however eager, should think twice, or three or four times, before sending in an application for an Ironman event. Earn your stripes in other distances for at least a year or two. Then you can go for the Big One.

Ironman Distance races are ideal for the following people:

- Triathletes who have completed several half-Ironman events and plan to increase their training to that next level
- Veteran triathletes who are looking for the ultimate challenge
- Triathletes who are willing to commit to 20 to 30 hours of training per week, possibly more

Tri-ing It Indoors

A great option for winter-bound triathletes or novices who fear open water is the indoor triathlon. Some indoor events keep all three activities inside, with the bike leg done on a stationary machine and the running portion on an indoor track or treadmill. Many indoor triathlons hold only the swimming portion in an indoor pool, with the bike and the run outside.

Indoor events also make great first triathlons and are a good way of starting off a triathlon season. They tend to be less intimidating because of the pool swim. Indoor events also usually have a small number of participants and are short in length (they normally don't go beyond the sprint distance).

Humble Beginnings for the Ironman Queen

If there were ever a motivating story for the beginner or new-comer to the sport, it's the tale of Ironman champion Paula Newby-Fraser. She grew up in Durban, South Africa, gradu-ated from college, and began working a nine-to-five job as a researcher in a property man-agement firm. Other than the occasional stroll around the block, Paula didn't exercise, and pretty soon, she grew concerned about her waistline.

"I was a couch potato," says Paula. "The most strenuous activity I participated in was walking to the beach and putting on suntan lotion." Spurred on by her friend, Adele, she began jogging three times a week. "Although the idea seemed preposterous, it came at a time when I was gaining weight. I was worried about the rubber tire inflating around my hips, so I gave her the nod." She soon grew to love it and joined a local running club that supported her with encouragement, training knowledge, and some competition in the form of weekly time-trial runs against the clock.

Several months later, after watching her boyfriend do a triathlon one summer, Paula became intrigued by the idea of completing one. In her first race, she placed second, and the rest, of course, is history. From such humble beginnings, Paula has won eight Ironman Triathlon championships and is considered by most to be the best female endurance athlete on the planet. "Looking back to that time period in my life when I took on my first formidable fitness goal of competing in the running club time-trial, I realize now that it had been the impetus that changed my whole outlook on life," says Paula.

Another Choice: The Triathlon Relay

Relay competition has become an increasingly popular offshoot of triathlon. Teams consist of a swimmer, a cyclist, and a runner who compete against other teams for the top total time. Many teams come close to bettering the professional finishing times. For many, team participation gives them a chance to have fun, improve fitness, and delve into the exciting world of multisport athletics without the full triathlon training schedule. For future triathletes, it provides a stepping stone to the full distance.

For many active people who train regularly in one discipline, relaying offers a comfortable vantage point from which to view triathlon fever. Although not every triathlon includes a relay competition, for the large events the relay has become a door by which those who want to feel out triathlons, those who thrive on team competition, and those with limitations can participate in an exciting multisport event. Among other advantages of relay divisions, they bring the spirit of team competition to an individual sport. Finally, relays are a means by which those who may think they could never do a triathlon might reconsider.

If you decide to do a relay, always try to do your best of the three events.

Chapter 2

Planning to Race

> "Plan your play, play your plan."
>
> *—John Schweizer*

Although most people enter multisports with the purpose of completing several triathlons, there are those that finish one and hang up their swim caps forever. They continue to cross-train, but they feel no need for competition, either against others or to better a personal best. But if, like me, you relish the energy and motivation of training for a race, then it's important to create a plan. Your goal can be anything from achieving a personal best to consistently training six days out of the week. However, setting your triathlon beacon on a race—whether it be a relay, sprint, or Olympic distance event—is a sure way to narrow your focus for a successful and satisfying experience.

Now that you have an idea of your triathlon choices, are you ready to set your sights on a particular race and make a plan? This chapter is interactive, with lots of questions and exercises designed to help you make some wise decisions. You'll need to sharpen your pencil because you'll fill in some blanks and do some writing. It'll be worth the effort—the answers you provide will lay the foundation for your triathlon adventure.

Step 1: Take a Personal Inventory

The distance you choose will depend upon your current fitness level, your experience with other sports, and your comfort level with open water swimming. Even if you've got your first triathlon under your belt and are looking to go faster or go longer, you'll still need to carefully consider these pre-planning issues. Take stock of where you stand in terms of fitness and skills by answering a few simple questions.

What Is My Cardiovascular Fitness Level Right Now?

Ask yourself, where am I right now? This question is important, and it's one worth taking some time to evaluate. In order to get where you want to go, you must first know where you are. By honestly evaluating your current fitness level, you avoid putting undue pressure on yourself by setting your initial sights too high. Putting pressure on yourself usually leads to injury from increasing mileage or intensity (or both) too quickly.

If you need to get in a lot of running and cycling, why not enjoy the process of building an endurance base by taking your time, gradually increasing your mileage, and maybe even doing a few running races or cycling rides in the meantime? It may take a little longer, but you'll find that by first honestly assessing your current fitness, you can create a training plan that is safe, systematic, and enjoyable. To help you gauge where you stand, photocopy and complete the Cardiovascular Fitness Worksheet on the next page.

How Are My Swimming Skills?

The nice thing about running and cycling is that neither takes the grace or coordination of a ballerina or the sensory skills of a marksman to execute. So, in most cases, the only skill that really requires polishing is front crawl swimming, an activity that requires some technical competence. (If the swim is very short, you can get by with a breaststroke or sidestroke—but I wouldn't recommend it.)

There's nothing quite like the feeling of coming out of the water in a race, although your legs may feel somewhat Gumby-like.

Cardiovascular Fitness Worksheet

Number of times you exercise in an aerobic activity per week: _____

Number of months you've maintained this exercise routine: _____

Rate your current cardiovascular fitness level on a 1 to 10 scale
(10 being the most fit): _____

Swimming Skills Worksheet

Can you swim the front crawl across a full pool length
without stopping? (circle one) **Yes   No**

If yes, write the number of pool lengths you can
currently complete without stopping: _____

Rate your skills in the front crawl on a 1 to 10 scale.
For example, if you find yourself unable to submerse
your head while swimming, a realistic assessment
might be 1. If you have a basic understanding of
proper technique, but have poor execution, rate yourself a 5. If your execution is fair to excellent, give
yourself a number between 6 and 10. _____

Open Water Worksheet

Have you ever swum in open water before? (circle one) **Yes   No**

Which statement best describes your comfort level in
open water? (check one)

_____ Extremely uncomfortable.   _____ Pretty comfortable.

_____ Mildly uncomfortable.   _____ My middle name is "Flipper."

_____ Okay.

If your swimming skills are not quite up to par, don't feel left out. Many triathletes don't swim like fish. Still, those who are serious about jumping into the sport and sticking around for awhile commit to improving, developing, or, in many cases, just learning to swim in the first place. For beginners, a local city college or YMCA program is the best place to start. If your swimming needs some serious work and it's already the middle of the triathlon racing season, why not set a target for next year and take beginning or intermediate swimming classes at your local city college during the fall and winter months? You could compete in duathlons for now and concentrate on getting ready for triathlon next year.

You should also ask yourself, "What is my comfort level in open water?" Does that question send a shiver down your spine? Well, again, you're not alone. Newcomers to the sport usually find open

Fish are harmless. They are more afraid of you than you are of them.

water swimming unnerving. If you're one of the many who feel like fish out of water in open water, then learning to swim in a lake or ocean may be your biggest challenge (unless your only triathlon aspiration is to complete an indoor triathlon). In part II of this book, I'll cover open water swimming in greater detail. For now, try to gauge where you stand (or tread water) right now by completing the Open Water Worksheet on page 20.

A Late Bloomer

Whoever said you can't teach an old dog new tricks never met Mike Greer. A highly-successful businessman, triathlon race director, and book author, Mike completed his first triathlon in 1984 at the age of 44. But long before he crossed his first triathlon finish line, Mike took stock of his skills and realized he needed to put in some serious swimming and cycling time. A veteran marathoner, his cardiovascular fitness and running base were solid. Yet his lack of swimming and cycling experience were serious weaknesses.

"I began to swim a lot because I had the endurance, but in hindsight, I should have found a coach to help me with my technique," says the Lubbock, Texas resident. "I read everything on swimming and cycling I could get my hands on and visited the local bike shops for advice and guidance on equipment and gearing. I spent a lot of time with other swimmers, cyclists, and triathletes, learning everything I could from them."

With this common sense approach to improve upon the skills he was lacking, he completed his first triathlon after a year of training. Since then, he has gotten heavily involved in the sport's political arena and is the race director of the popular Buffalo Springs Lake Triathlon, a half-Ironman event in Lubbock. As of the end of 1997, he had 162 triathlon finishes to his credit, including several Ironman distance races. "I'm slow, painfully slow, but I can keep going," Mike says of his race times. "I love triathlon, the people, and the lifestyle. It's a helluva deal."

Step 2: Set a Realistic Goal

Have you ever had the experience of striving for something and finding out down the road that you don't have the time, energy, or motivation to follow through until completion? Or worse, have you ever exhausted yourself physically, mentally, and spiritually to accomplish a goal, only to realize that you didn't enjoy one single bit of it?

If you want to succeed in the multisport arena, you've got to set a realistic goal. Now, "realistic" is different for everyone, and what may be realistic for one person is totally insane for somebody else. All of us have unique responsibilities in terms of work, family, and society. The trick is to determine a commitment level that will contribute to a balanced lifestyle and not cause stress.

You may have multiple goals, but the more focused you are, the better your chances. There's nothing wrong with having multiple goals, as long as you are realistic about your time and capabilities. For now, why not just focus on one chief goal? With that in mind, let's move forward through a few questions that will help determine what that goal will be.

What Distance Is Right for Me?

Keeping in mind your current fitness level, refer back to chapter 1 and reread the descriptions of the four predominant distance categories. Don't make the mistake of setting your race goal too high above your current fitness level, especially if your base training has been minimal. (Base training is a term I'll get into later on in the training chapters. For now, just realize that this term describes a fitness foundation of regular aerobic exercise in an endurance sport over an extended period of time.)

Are you willing to put in the training that is required before attempting a sprint or Olympic distance triathlon? If not, what about a relay? If you have a specific race coming up soon that you are thinking of doing, do you have enough time to train? For example, if you come from a running background, but your longest run thus far has been six miles, and your cycling and swimming have been nil, the half-Ironman triathlon next month is not realistic.

Besides your current fitness, consider how much time you have to train, how training will affect your family life, career, or both.

Although a sprint distance requires a relatively small amount of training, training for an Ironman can be like taking on another full-time job. Complete the Distance Worksheet to determine which triathlon distance best suits you now.

Distance Worksheet

Approximate number of hours per week you can commit
to triathlon training: _____

Triathlon distance that is right for you, based on training
times given in chapter 1? (check one)

_____	Relay	_____	Half-Ironman*
_____	Sprint	_____	Ironman*
_____	Olympic		

*If one of these distances was your choice, what will be the effect on your family
life, career, or both? _____

_____

Which Race Should I Do?

Now comes the moment for you to put it all on the line and choose a specific race as your triathlon goal. Check the appendix for a list of multisport publications and Web sites that list races in your area. Ask your triathlete friends which races they would recommend. Ideally, you should be looking for a race that gives you ample time to get up to speed, depending on the inventory you took in step 1. Don't plan for a race that will rush your training. If it's already late in the triathlon racing season in your area of the world, plan for next season.

Look for the following information when reviewing races:

- Number of years the race has been around
- USA Triathlon sanctioned (not an absolute necessity, but the top races usually are)

- What your triathlon friends (the ones who have done the race) say about it
- Swim course safety, such as the number of lifeguards and how clearly you can see the swim buoys
- Aid stations on the run course (and on the bike course for Olympic distances or longer)
- Race application fee
- Post-race food and activities
- Available lodging and accommodations in the race area (if staying overnight)

If you're new to the sport, you should keep things as simple as possible for your first few races. Local events within driving distance are better than having to deal with air travel and taking apart your bike to fit into a bicycle case. (Although the multisport air travel vacation is a great little getaway for the veteran, it's not the best choice for the beginner.) Small races are better than circus-like mass starts, and rural venues are usually much less intimidating than metro madness. The following worksheet will help you narrow your choices.

What Do I Want to Accomplish?

There are three reasons to race: to finish, to improve, or to win. Unless you're a professional athlete or top age grouper, your goal will likely be to finish or improve upon previous finishing times. Ask yourself, "Is this a race I just want to finish, or am I willing to put in the necessary higher level of training to set a personal best?"

If your next triathlon will be your first ever, then it's best to set an objective of simply finishing. (If it's your first race, it'll be a personal best anyway, no matter what your finishing time, so you may as well just concentrate on finishing.) By taking this approach, you'll take a lot of pressure off yourself. You've got enough to worry about with your first race; don't create undue tension by demanding that you cross the finish line at a set time.

However, if you've done a triathlon or two and are looking to improve upon your previous times, that's fine too. The forthcoming chapters will provide you with all the information you need to get more familiar with the equipment and training techniques you need

Race Selection Worksheet

Taking into account my open water comfort level and swimming ability, I would prefer an

_____ indoor swim.   _____ open water ocean swim.

_____ open water lake swim.

I would prefer a race

_____ within driving distance.   _____ that I would travel to by air.

I would prefer a

_____ small race with less than   _____ a big race with more than 500
500 participants.   participants.

I would prefer a race in

_____ an urban setting.   _____ a rural setting.

My ideal bike and run course would be

_____ flat as a pancake.   _____ very hilly.

_____ somewhat hilly.

Given the above criteria, list a few races that you might be interested in doing:

1.

2.

3.

From the preceding list, which race takes place at a time of the year that will give you the ideal amount of training time to ensure that you are fully prepared to complete the event?

Race name: _____

Race date:_____   Months to train: _____

to bump up your speed or take on a longer distance. Fill out the Objectives Worksheet on page 28 to help provide focus to your plan.

Why Do I Want to Do This Race?

Most people don't take the time to document their motivation behind a goal. Though they may spend an evening writing up a training schedule or goal chart, which they proudly post on their refrigerator door for all to see, they don't bother to examine and write down the reason or reasons why they are embarking on this training program.

Goals, in themselves, are very important. But if you don't have a clear idea of why you are setting those goals, you may find your motivation waning at critical junctures in your training (such as those cold and rainy mornings when you just don't feel like getting into the pool and practicing swim drills). Once you've committed yourself to a race goal, take the necessary step of documenting— whether in a diary, journal, or triathlon training log—your true motivation in striving for this goal (more on a triathlon training log later). Complete the Motivation Exercise on page 28, and then keep it someplace where you will see it constantly, perhaps posted along-side your training schedule or list of goals on your refrigerator door.

I know it sounds like a bit much, but motivational experts agree that the more firepower you have behind your goals, the more likely it is that you'll do the work and have the self-discipline needed to succeed. By listing the numerous benefits and reasons for desiring a goal, you'll build up the motivational energy to get you through those tough training runs. I recommend 50 reasons as a minimum, but if you can stretch it to 100 reasons, you'll be so fired up, you won't be able to wait until your next swim, ride, or run.

Don't just look at the physical and external reasons. Point your emotional compass inward and analyze your feelings about this goal. One note: the longer your list, the harder this exercise becomes. But press on—usually it's those last few reasons that cut to the heart of your motivation. You'll know that you're doing a good job with this exercise if you have to use the back of this sheet to finish your list.

Step 3: Set Up Your Training Calendar and Log

Now that you know where you are and where you want to go, the final step is to get some things on paper (as if you haven't already worn out your no. 2 pencil). Setting up your training calendar and

Objectives Worksheet

What do I hope to accomplish?

_____ Finish the race

_____ Improve upon a previous triathlon performance

My previous triathlon performance: _____

_____ Win the race

_____ Overall

_____ My age group

Motivation Exercise

List 50 to 100 benefits of achieving your triathlon goal.

triathlon training log can be the two most important actions you take, perhaps more important than any swim intervals, long rides, or morning runs you do.

Your Triathlon Training Calendar

Your training calendar can be a preprinted calendar, a poster board, an appointment book, or a calendar software program that prints out customized monthly grids. Whatever form it takes, the main requirement is that you have enough room to write down your workouts for each day leading up to your race goal.

Your training calendar should also be something on paper, as opposed to just on a computer screen. Although a software program is great for creating customized calendars, make sure it also has the capability to print out monthly grids. You want your training calendar be within plain sight, not hidden away somewhere on a computer hard drive. Dedicate a space for your calendar—someplace that you know you'll see every day. Once you've chosen your calendar and picked a place to put it, it's time to make the commitment and put pen to calendar (scary, huh?).

Work Your Way Back From Race Day

The first thing you want to do is to mark down your race goal on your training calendar. How much time does that give you to train properly? Again, take into account your current fitness level and skills. If you need to reassess your race goal and set your target on something more realistic, now is the time to do it.

Divide Your Calendar Into Phases

Although I get into much more training detail in part II, you'll need to know a little bit about what experts consider to be the optimum way to train. Training in phases or cycles has long been considered the best way to condition your body to the rigors of endurance exercise safely and effectively. Each phase has a very specific objective, and the workouts are thoughtfully designed to fulfill that objective.

Coaches and fitness experts don't always agree on the exact number of phases and objectives (largely because training differs so much between sports and elite athletes require much more complex training plans). However, for the multisport novice or future triathlete looking for that first finish line crossing, there are some basic phases that should be integrated into your training calendar. Following is a very brief description of each of these phases.

If you feel you have a good handle on how much time you need to devote to each phase after reading this section, go ahead and divide your training calendar accordingly. (Otherwise, wait until you review chapter 7 for more specific recommendations.) If you're a neat freak, you may even want to use color highlighters to block off phases, using a different color for each one. Don't worry about writing down specific workouts; we'll get to that later. For now, just get familiar with the different phases, objectives, and estimated time frames.

The Initiation Phase (Beginners Only)

Objective: To learn a new activity never or rarely performed before.
Estimated time: Depends on level of inexperience. If you are learning to swim the front crawl, this phase can take three months or more.

The Base Phase

Objective: To create a foundation of training with gradual, safe adaptation to a physical activity.
Estimated time: Three to six months, depending on current conditioning, skills, and the distance for which you are training.

The Speed and Technique Phase

Objective: To increase both the pace you can maintain and the efficiency of your exercise.
Estimated time: Three weeks to several months, depending on current conditioning and performance goals.

The Race Simulation Phase

Objective: To boost race day confidence by completing workouts similar to what you will be doing in the event.
Estimated time: One to two months, depending on current conditioning and race goals.

The Tapering Phase

Objective: To feel mentally and physically fresh for a race.
Estimated time: One to four weeks prior to your event, depending on the distance. Sprint distance races usually only require a week of tapering.

Your Training Log

When you think of a journal or log, the first thought that might occur is sentimentality about the past. Part of the value of keeping such records is to remind you of your accomplishments, but keeping a record of your triathlon training and racing has more practical applications as well.

If you don't keep a training log, you are ignoring an opportunity to avoid possible injury and improve your performance. Maintaining an accurate log of your daily and weekly workouts is one of the best ways to keep on track. A log that chronicles the variables that affect your energy level and performance can help you achieve your triathlon goal.

There are many handy preprinted training logs that you can purchase. Some have motivating quotes and pictures and space for many variables. If you're a computer geek, several workout log programs are available on the market.

There's no one way to keep a training log. Whatever you think are the most applicable variables are fine. To help create an individualized log with a spiral notebook and a ruler, here are some suggested variables to make columns for:

• **Hours slept.** Current research suggests moderate sleep deprivation has little effect on performance during the adrenaline high of competition. Still, that ragged feeling during a three-mile training jog may be the result of too little snooze time.

• **Waking pulse.** Record your beats per minute when you awake, preferably while you're still in bed. An increase of more than three or four beats can signal overtraining.

• **Distances or time.** Tracking correct distances or workout time can keep you honest. It is also your most reliable measuring stick to check your progress.

• **Time of day.** Studies show that energy levels fluctuate during the day according to many factors that are unique to individuals. As long as all other variables remain the same, you can pinpoint your peak time of day for a workout.

• **Intensity.** Use descriptive terms or a 1 to 10 number scale, with 1 being very easy and 10 being extremely difficult. Monitoring intensity levels is a key in avoiding too many back-to-back killer workouts (or in avoiding that crippling disease, couchus potatoeus).

• **Feelings.** Though many things can affect your mood, a change in mood is sometimes a precursor to sickness and an indication of overtraining. For example, irritability is an early sign that you're pushing yourself too hard.

• **Injury flags.** Pay close attention to any unusual pain, especially around the joints where most injuries occur. Note any such aches and pains in your log.

• **Weight.** Get on the scale in the morning, after you've relieved yourself. A 3 percent or more loss of body weight may mean you've lost too much fluid as a result of dehydration. Take an easy day or, better yet, a day off.

• **Weather.** If you are easily affected by heat, cold, humidity, or other weather variables, keep track of these conditions.

• **Notes.** Perhaps the best part about keeping a training log is flipping back to read about that special swim, ride, run, or race.

Chapter 3

Getting the Right Stuff

> "You can't always get what you want, but if you try sometimes, you just might find you get what you need."
>
> —*Rolling Stones*

Almost a decade ago, the Triathlon Federation/USA (now USA Triathlon) conducted a survey and found that the average amount of money triathletes shell out a year for equipment purchases was about $2,011. The survey also concluded (rather smugly) that most triathletes can afford it. The average income of triathletes was estimated to be over $50,000 a year, with 23.6 percent making more than $70,000.

No doubt, those figures are probably outdated. (USA Triathlon has no current estimates.) With the gain in popularity of multisports and triathletes becoming less of an elitist group, the average income has probably gone down. But the cost of proper equipment has certainly gone up. Where does that leave the blue-collar triathlete who has to make a decision between buying a wetsuit and paying the rent? Unless you're among the 23.6 percent riding high with plenty of disposable income, you'll want to get the most from your hard-earned dollar.

The key to getting the right gear for triathlon and not taking out a second mortgage on your house is making smart choices. Part of being smart means not spending a lot of money on a sport that you're only beginning to explore. Put away the credit cards; there's no need to make any rash and expensive purchases without fully exploring your options and understanding what you need versus what you may want (or what other triathletes think is cool to have).

In this chapter, we'll take a look at the triathlon equipment you'll need for a season full of multisport action, along with estimated cost ranges. We'll take it one sport at a time and cover the basics, as well as some not-so-basic stuff that you may want to consider down the line. You'll find that if you discard the bells and whistles (or in this case, neon and iridium), you won't have to deal with a foreclosure notice.

Swimming Stuff

As is the case with much of the equipment we'll discuss, you shouldn't skimp on swimming apparel and accessories. Buy quality brands that will last you over the long haul.

Swimsuits

If you don't already own a swimsuit, that's your first order of business. Though a great variety of swimsuits are available, there are a few special considerations you might want to ponder.

First, conventional swimsuits are not designed for bicycle riding or running. As a result, they offer little bicycle padding and running comfort. They are generally very thin and tight, which is fine for lap swimming, but doesn't help your sore butt on a thin bike saddle. (It's a personal choice, but in sprint and Olympic distance races, most triathletes compete in their swimsuits. There's nothing wrong, however, with donning a pair of bike shorts in the transition area if you prefer. Chapter 10 has more info on transition choices.)

The lack of padding in conventional swimsuits could lead to saddle soreness and the tightness could lead to chafing during the run. In addition, a conventional swimsuit may wear out much quicker or stretch out along the gluteus maximus so that you look like you were last in the port-a-potty line. Look for swimsuits specifically designed for multisports. Some have a thin layer of padding and a narrow design for less chafing along the groin. Some even have a little pocket for your energy bar.

Second, if you're training with baggy swimming trunks, leave those for water slide time with the kids and get serious with a narrow-style, racing-cut swimsuit. As you'll learn later, it's important to be slippery in the water, and you might be surprised how much a baggy pair of swim trunks can make you drag in the pool.

Estimated cost for a triathlon racing swimsuit: $20 to $40 for men's and $40 to $80 for women's.

Swimming Goggles

Triathletes are divided on the issue of goggles. Although some buy the top-of-the-line brand, others feel that all they need is something to put between their eyes and the water. When choosing how much to spend on goggles, consider whether you will be wearing contact lenses during your swim. If you can't afford to have your vision washed out with the tide, spend some money for a pair of quality goggles that is durable, resists leaking, and can't be kicked off your face too easily (which is always a possibility in an open water swim).

I recommend that you spend the money for a top-of-the-line pair. When you consider how important goggles are, especially for "water-challenged" triathletes who don't care to have any surprises on the swim (such as annoying leaks or goggle bands that snap), then spending a little bit more is worth the price.

Estimated cost for swimming goggles: $10 to $50.

Wetsuits

A wetsuit offers safety, speed, and warmth to the novice open water swimmer. But do you need one if you just want to finish your first sprint distance triathlon? Probably not. For longer distances and colder open water courses, the importance of having a wetsuit increases.

Also, if you're testing the triathlon waters and aren't quite sure you like the sport enough to get good use out of such a purchase, better hold off. Though a wetsuit is an excellent investment for the serious triathlete intent on getting mileage from this neoprene magic, consider buying one only when you have no doubt that you will keep tri-ing for many years and many open water swims to come.

Wetsuit Benefits

The benefits of swimming with a wetsuit depend on a myriad of individual factors, such as percentage of body fat, stroke efficiency, body temperature, and a host of other variables. However, there are four areas of consistent return on a wetsuit investment:

• **Buoyancy.** Wetsuits come in a variety of thicknesses, but all have the advantage of lifting you higher above the water and keeping your body balanced. This advantage is especially helpful to novice swimmers who have poor technique and tend to drag the lower body in the water.

• **Warmth.** Hypothermia is a constant danger in chilly open waters. Wetsuits keep you warm by initially trapping a thin layer of water between the fabric and your skin. This layer warms you and keeps you safe and comfortable. (A properly fitted wetsuit ensures that this layer stays intact.)

• **Energy conservation.** With the increase in buoyancy, you won't have to work as hard to get ahead. That means you shouldn't have to take as many strokes to move through the water. So your stroke count, as well as your energy expenditure, should decrease.

• **Speed.** Though the less-experienced swimmer will benefit much more than the veteran, more efficient swimmer, wetsuits will help bring that swim time down.

The Wetsuit Cut for You

The wetsuit style or cut that you choose will fall under one of three categories: full-cut, sleeveless, or the most recently introduced short-cut. Your choice should be determined by the environment in which you swim and some personal preferences.

- **Full-cut wetsuits**. Full-cut wetsuits cover your arms and legs and are the warmest and most buoyant. So why look elsewhere? Not so fast. Full-cut wetsuits can be uncomfortable and take longer to get out of, so the added benefits may well be offset by slapstick maneuvers in the transition area. In addition, they can significantly change your swim mechanics. Wetsuit manufacturers are continually striving to improve full-cut designs so they are more comfortable and less

Full-cut wetsuits may take longer to peel off, but are recommended for colder water swims to help avoid hypothermia.

taxing on transitions. For swims in very cold water, full-cut wetsuits are by far the most appropriate. They are also the most expensive.

• **Sleeveless wetsuits.** Sleeveless wetsuits are the most popular choice for triathletes. For beefy, muscle-bound types, they are the obvious choice. The sleeveless design still provides you with most of the warming benefits, but leaves you with complete freedom of movement in the arms, a less harrowing transition, and a slightly smaller bill.

• **Short-cut wetsuits.** In recent years, wetsuit manufacturers have introduced short-cut wetsuits that mimic a design surfers have been using for years. A short-cut wetsuit is sleeveless and extends only to the knees. By sacrificing warmth and buoyancy, you gain in the transition area with quick exits. In addition, the minimum coverage provides a more natural, less rubber glove-like feel for the swim leg.

Wetsuit Shopping Tips

Are you convinced that you need to get a wetsuit? I'm not surprised. Most newcomers to the sport, especially those who dread open water swimming, gladly plunk down a hundred or so bucks for a little more confidence in the water.

The single greatest consideration when shopping for a wetsuit is fit. The key? Take your time. Until you find a wetsuit that fits you like a second skin, don't be satisfied with anything less. Fit should be tight, but not to the point where you find motion constricted, or can't breathe normally. Pay close attention to how the wetsuit fits in the arm holes (for sleeveless designs) and neck area. These are the two locations where unwanted excess water is most likely to enter.

The main fabric in wetsuits is neoprene, a soft rubber that is comfortable, resilient, and a good insulator. The thickness of most wetsuits varies. The smarter designs use a combination of thicknesses within the same wetsuit to facilitate both buoyancy and

Speed Demon Fact

Depending on conditions, your technique, and the type of wetsuit, you can shave anywhere from one to five minutes off your time during an Olympic distance open water swim (1.5 kilometers) with a wetsuit.

flexibility. For example, many manufacturers use a thick five millimeters of neoprene in the chest and leg areas for greater buoyancy and a level swimming position. Yet in sleeves, neck, and arm holes, a thinner three millimeters of neoprene allow for greater flexibility. The thickness you choose should depend on your swimming experience, where you swim (cold or very cold water), and whether you have a tendency to drag.

Of course, cost is certainly a factor. Most full-cut wetsuits surpass the $200 mark, sleeveless wetsuits sell for just under that, and the short-cut designs usually hover around the $100 to $150 range.

Estimated cost for a wetsuit: $100 to $250.

Bicycle Stuff

If you've only recently been bitten by the triathlon bug, the very first, most obvious symptom is an inexplicable need to visit the nearest bicycle shop. Once there, your symptoms may progress toward making out a check for a thousand bucks, or worse, taking out the plastic. Hold on there. You may not need to shell out four figures at this point.

If you currently own a bicycle and just want to finish your first triathlon, you may be able to get by with what you have until you're sure you'll be a lifelong multisport maniac. It's not uncommon for beginners to use a beat-up old road bike or a fat-tire mountain bike for their first event, and there's absolutely nothing wrong with that. However, if you don't have a bicycle (or can't borrow one), then you have no alternative but to look into buying a triathlon bicycle. Also, if you've done a few triathlons and are looking for some advice on making your first serious multisport bicycle purchase, the following sections provide some guidelines for you.

Tri-Bikes, Step by Step

Making your entry into the complicated world of cycling equipment can be expensive and intimidating. Somewhere among the splashy neon colors, shiny components, and black rubber is what you need. Without some basic knowledge, a good understanding of your current needs, and a clear vision of what lurks on your triathlon horizon, there's a strong chance that you'll purchase the wrong bicycle.

For most triathletes, their bicycle is their most prized possession. You may want to ask before borrowing one from a friend.

Fear not. Here's a step-by-step guide to making that first big multisport purchase, with advice from triathlon bicycle dealers, manufacturers, and coaches. Add to that some tales of woe from professionals who can tell you (through their experience) what *not* to do when you're making that big purchase, and you've got no reason to panic.

Step 1: Set a Budget

Walking into a bicycle shop with no plan can mean walking away with no money. Although most bike dealers will not deliberately take advantage of an eager first-time buyer, by setting a budget you are taking the first step toward controlling a situation that may seem uncontrollable.

A cautionary word about overemphasizing equipment is warranted. "Your best bet is buying a reasonably priced, entry-level bike with a clip-on aero bar," says cycling coach Bob Langan. "It all comes to this: it's not the seconds equipment will save you; it's the minutes a good aerodynamic position and proper training will."

How much will you spend on your first triathlon bike? Generally speaking, prices range between $800 to $1,200 for an entry-level racing bicycle. Of course, the sky's the limit on how much you *can* spend, but spending more than $1,200 is risky for two reasons: 1) you may not know what you need; 2) you may think you know what you need, but you may be wrong.

Does that mean you should go the other way and get the cheapest two-wheeler you see on the dealer floor? You don't want to go that route either, according to Dan Siever, bicycle shop salesman at The Wheel Thing in LaGrange, Illinois: "A lot of people want to start with the bottom-of-the-line and end up spending about $300 on something that becomes obsolete really quick. I think it's better to buy a bicycle at the upper end of what you can afford than to save a few hundred dollars and end up paying for it down the road when you have to replace it because it's not good enough for racing."

If you're showing some hesitation in plunking down so much money for a bicycle, perhaps it's because you're new to the sport and are not sure how deep (physically and financially) you want to go. That's the dilemma professional duathlete Liz Downing faced the first time she walked into a bicycle shop after doing her first few races with some moderate degree of success. "I had no idea I was going to do this well in duathlon, but when I made my decision to buy a racing bike, price was a major factor," says Liz Downing. "I think that above $800 you're going to get a lot more for your money. Of course, once you reach a certain point, the differences diminish. There's not that much difference between a $5,000 and a $6,000 bike."

Step 2: Don't Forget Accessories

One common mistake is excluding accessories from the budget. You should earmark at least $200 to $400 for accessories, more if you intend to purchase optional equipment such as a fancy aerodynamic disk, tri-spoke, or deep rim wheels. Some of the more basic bicycle accessories include the following:

- Frame pump
- Patch kit

- Spare tubes
- Helmet
- Clothing (shorts, jerseys, jacket)
- Gloves
- Cycling shoes (optional)
- Clipless pedals (optional)
- Aero bars (optional)
- Computer (optional)
- Sunglasses (optional)

As you can imagine, your $700 bicycle purchase can run well into four figures with the addition of these or any other accessories. Is all this stuff really necessary? Most of it is. You can't race without a helmet, and you need the additional comfort and safety that cycling shorts, jerseys, gloves, and all the other necessities afford you.

If you intend to transport your bicycle in your car, a roof-mounted bicycle rack can run you well over $250. A less expensive alternative is a trunk-mounted rack. Still cheaper is taking the wheels off your bike and throwing it in the back seat or trunk.

In recent years, many bicycle manufacturers have included clipless pedals, contraptions that attach you to the bike for an efficient, more comfortable pedal stroke, as basic equipment on entry-level road bike models. This addition will save you close to $100 dollars in

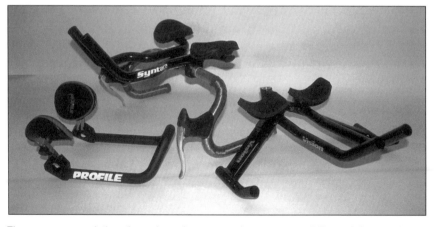

There are many varieties of aero bars, from a complete system, to "clip-ons" that attach to existing handlebars.

money you may have earmarked for this accessory. (If the bicycle you're interested in doesn't include clipless pedals, it's time to start negotiating with your dealer.) Though many people fear being attached to a bicycle in this way, the nice thing about clipless pedals is that you can get out of them at any time simply by extending your heel outward. Cycling shoes are designed for use with clipless pedals. Cycling shoes are stiff and transfer energy much more directly to the bicycle than do rubber pedals or toe straps.

Aero bars, although not mandatory, do help you slice through the wind significantly. Better aerodynamics with aero bars increase your speed and help you save energy for the run. As you train for longer distances, this accessory will definitely fall out of the "optional" category and into the "mandatory" list.

Speed Demon Fact

If you recall, Greg Lemond's historic victory in the 1989 Tour de France came as a direct result of the performance advantage of his "triathlon" aero bars. Wind tunnel testing has shown an estimated average time savings of five minutes during an Olympic distance bike leg (40 kilometers) when a cyclist maintains an aerodynamic position on aero bars. Other studies have also shown that cyclists in a proper aerodynamic position are more relaxed and experience decreased heart rates.

Step 3: Understand the Choices and Know What You Need

The general idea is to spend wisely, and that means making a purchase that satisfies your present need for a good racing bicycle and is versatile enough to last. Buying an entry-level racing bike that is upgradable can save you a lot of time and money in the long term.

For example, Ken Souza's first duathlon bicycle was a Nishiki International he bought back in 1982 for a scant $175. Though the bicycle served its initial purpose, it was a touring model (a bicycle designed primarily for casual riding) that Souza quickly outgrew. Yet the persistent former duathlon king continued to pour money into a pocket full of holes. "It was ironic. I was spending all this money trying to upgrade, trying to save a few dollars by not buying a racing bike. I could have brought a real racing bike sooner if I hadn't tried so hard to upgrade a bike that wasn't worth it."

Souza's solution to his novice woes was one that you might want to consider if the opportunity arises: "I bought a used racing bike—a Vitus carbon fiber—from ex-pro Mark Montgomery. I think that's one of the smartest things a beginner can do. You'll get top-of-the-line gear, you can get a great deal, and it's usually not beat up."

Again, before you plunk down any money on a high-tech piece of equipment, ask yourself: "Just how seriously am I going to take this triathlon stuff anyway?" "You have to be honest with yourself," says Steve Hed, wheel manufacturer and bicycle guru. "How many hours are you going to spend in the saddle? Are you going to stick with it, or are you going to spend all this money and give it up after one season? Do you want to be competitive, or are you just doing this for fun?"

When you finally look at some entry-level racing bikes, you'll find there are several options available, and several common questions arise. The dealer might bring up these questions, or you may have already begun to ask them:

• **What's the difference between a road bike and a triathlon bike?** Although a bicycle strictly designed for the time-trial situation of a triathlon is somewhat different from a traditional road racing bicycle, most entry-level road racing models will make excellent bicycles for the beginning triathlete making his or her first bicycle purchase. (Later on, you can easily upgrade an entry-level road bike with more serious equipment such as aero bars, disk wheels or deep rim wheels, or some lightweight replacement parts.) Typically, once you get into the more specialized high-level triathlon bikes, such as those made of titanium and other exotic frame materials, some features such as steeper seat tube angles and 26-inch wheels delineate the triathlon bicycle from the road bicycle.

If all the options confuse you, don't feel too bad—even the pros have a tough time finally settling with the right ride. For example, duathlete Liz Downing's very first triathlon steed was a Schwinn Varsity, a 70-pound bomber that gives new meaning to the term "heavy metal." Though that was soon supplanted with a Nishiki, then later a Raleigh, she has finally settled on a Quintana Roo, a bicycle specifically designed for triathletes. On the next page are two examples of triathlon bikes—one entry-level and one high-end.

• **Should I get clinchers or sew-up tires?** This question may very well be irrelevant if your first tri-bike purchase is in the $1,200 range; most entry-level racing bicycles come standard with clinchers, which are wheels with inner tubes and a rubber tire that snaps into a

An entry-level bike may include add-ons such as aero bars, clipless pedals, and aerodynamic wheels. This Fuji model retails for just over $1,000.

This Zipp is a high-end triathlon bike with a beam design for better aerodynamics and comfort. Beam bikes range from $2,000 to $5,000.

U-shaped rim. Sew-ups are self-contained tires (with no inner tube) glued onto a flat rim.

Though sew-ups are the tire of choice for professional racers, clincher tire technology has made it possible to get nearly the same feel, low rolling resistance, and smooth cornering. Unfortunately, many entry-level racing bicycles come standard with low-quality clincher tires that have a high degree of rolling resistance and are puncture-prone. Any reputable dealer will agree to substitute stock tires with a top-of-the-line tire such as a Michelin, Specialized, or Continental without adding more than $30 to $50 dollars to the price tag.

• **What's the best frame material: steel, aluminum, or carbon?** Although titanium and other new high-tech frame materials are way out of the $1,200 range, the selection of affordable bicycles made of steel, aluminum, and now carbon is starting to widen. Each frame material has subtle, but distinct, characteristics that really come down to riding preference. One camp of cyclists prefers the flexible ride of a shock absorbing carbon frame, but another camp would rather feel the stiff transfer of power that a steel frame can give you. For an even stiffer ride, there's the lightweight advantage of aluminum. Find your preference by taking a few bicycles with different frame materials for a test ride at your local bicycle shop.

• **What brand should I choose?** There is a plethora of bicycle manufacturers to choose from and most shops carry several different brands. Like an audiophile in a quality stereo shop, a triathlete in a good bike shop will find endless options that will do the job and minimal differences between them.

If you can't decide which brand to go with, Liz Downing suggests some investigative snooping at your next triathlon; look at what some top age groupers are riding. If something catches your eye, fits in your price range, and the stud or studette who's riding it has already showered by the time you cross the finish line, chances are it will be a good choice for you.

Step 4: Find a Good Dealer

Where you decide to buy your bicycle is almost as important as the purchase itself. Without advice, service, and accessories to back up your investment, you won't get as much enjoyment out of your new ride.

So do you go with a local bicycle shop or choose a discount mail firm? Before you take out the credit card and decide to phone in your order for a fast-looking road bike on a catalog page, think again. Though getting a bike through a mail-order company may seem like the wise thing to do, by forgoing a trip to your local bicycle shop, you're cutting yourself off from a wealth of knowledge, information, and personal service.

If you've already decided on a particular brand, there are a few benefits in going to a shop that has the biggest investment in that line. The salespeople will know more about them and will likely offer you the best deal. If you're not sure who's got the biggest investment, call the manufacturer and ask him which local dealer he recommends—the representative you speak to will probably send you to the one he or she knows will do the best job.

Step 5: Buy a Bike That Fits You

Though getting "fitted" may seem more of an appropriate term when going to the tailor, it's just as important when buying a bicycle. Considering all the miles you and your trusty steed will share, a properly fitted bicycle can mean the difference between limping or dashing through a run "leg."

How important is fit in relation to performance? According to John Cobb, a Louisiana dealer who has done extensive wind tunnel tests, plenty important: "You can take a gifted cyclist and put him on a bike that doesn't fit him, and he'll get beat to death by a much lesser athlete on a good-fitting bike."

The best way to ensure that you are properly fitted on your bicycle is to find a dealer willing to spend some time with you and take a look at your position on the bike. By setting up your bicycle on an indoor trainer and taking a few measurements, a good dealer with knowledge of proper bike fit can make a big difference on how comfortable and efficient you are in the saddle.

Step 6: Use Your Investment

There are probably as many newly purchased entry-level racing bikes gathering dust in the garage as there are wedding dresses tucked away in the attic. Buying proper clothing, learning about bicycle mechanics, getting involved in group rides, and setting goals is as essential to your triathlon success as making a wise initial investment.

Proper maintenance of your bike is vital too. First on your list of things to learn should be how to change a flat. Have someone you know show you how, or ask your bicycle dealer. Though gearing and your derailleur may seem intimidating, learn some simple techniques to help keep your components clean and in sound working condition. Your dealer may offer maintenance workshops and classes.

Estimated cost of an entry-level triathlon bicycle: $800 to $1,200.

Racing Tip

Prepare yourself for the possibility of a flat during a race the same as you would for a long training ride. Many beginners make the mistake of "lightening up the load" during a race and forgo the frame pump, spare tubes, and tire levers for the hundredth of a second they might save with less weight. Don't do it. Although some races do have bicycle support that will assist you in changing a flat, most do not.

Running Stuff

Although certainly not as pricey a sport as cycling, running can get expensive if you let it. Between the latest high-tech jackets, running shorts, socks and shoes, well, you could be looking at several hundred dollars. Is there any need to spend that much in preparing for your triathlon adventure? Again, probably not. Your old, worn-out windbreaker and the high-school gym shorts with the holes in them will do just fine for now. But there is one piece of running equipment you definitely don't want to skimp on: shoes.

About six years ago, I hobbled into a medical tent with blood bruises on two of my toes after completing my first marathon. Being the inexperienced runner that I was, I had done the Chicago Marathon in running shoes that didn't fit quite right. In hindsight, I don't think the shoes I ran in during that first 26.2-miler were a size too large or too small for me. They just weren't the right shoes for my feet.

If you come from a running background, you've probably found a good shoe that works for you. Once you've found a running shoe that provides just the right amount of cushioning, support, stability, and comfort, then keep buying 'em. It's not a bad idea to buy several pairs and stock up because shoe manufacturers regularly discontinue models. (If you are new to running, you'll find some practical advice on choosing the right shoe in chapter 6.)

No matter what running background you come from, if you haven't found the perfect shoe, find a local running specialty shop as fast as your feet will take you there. As with cycling, you will greatly benefit by picking the brain of people who have specialized knowledge. The personnel at running store specialty shops can guide you in purchasing the right shoe for your unique feet. Most times, you'll find friendly, knowledgeable people who are runners themselves and like nothing better than to turn you on to the right shoe.

The Frugal Triathlete

In this day of instant financing and tempting credit card limits, it's easy to get swept away in the triathlon craze and plunk down a few thousand bucks on a shiny, cool triathlon bike with all the latest gadgetry. But Butch Forsyth took the road less traveled—he decided from the onset that (like the famous muffler commercial) he just wasn't gonna pay full price.

"I've been interested in doing triathlons for a few years," says the 33-year-old from Salinas, California, who completed his first triathlon in March of 1997. "But every time I walked into a bike shop, I was just blown away by all these high prices. I really couldn't afford a new bike, and I wasn't about to charge it and end up making payments for years, especially since I hadn't even done my first race and wasn't sure I'd be doing more."

He found a solution when he walked into a shop selling a used road bike for about $500, a price that was more in his range. He negotiated a three-month layaway plan, and so far, he's found his used bike to be an excellent investment. He's also applied this same common sense approach to other triathlon gear, buying a used wetsuit at a Play It Again Sports® store for half the price of a new one and purchasing his running shoes when they're on sale. Butch estimates his total triathlon gear expenses have been under $750, compared to USA Triathlon's outdated (and no doubt low) estimate of $2,011 for triathlon equipment purchases. That's a savings of $1,261!

"You don't need a ton of money or an expensive triathlon bike to do your first few triathlons," advises Butch. "There's a lot of great deals out there in used equipment and road bikes. Even better, if you have friends that do triathlons, you can always borrow equipment."

Of course, you'll save money by going through mail-order catalogs or to a large sporting goods chain. But if you don't know exactly what shoe is best for your foot, running style, and the goal you've set, then buying a running shoe without the guidance of a runner at a local specialty shop is like taking a shot in the dark.

Many specialty shops are also much more willing than sporting good chains to let you take a test drive, either on an in-store treadmill or around the block. It's a very important thing to do because you need to feel how your foot fits the shoe during the motion of running. Although the shoe may feel great walking around, running is the best indicator of a good fit.

Be prepared when you visit your local running shoe store. The more information you can provide to the salesman/runner about your running and goals, the better he or she can match you to the right pair of shoes. Here are a few things you should talk about with your specialty store salesperson:

- Miles per week you run
- Type of surface you usually run on (asphalt, grass, trails, gravel)
- Type of running injuries you've experienced in the past

Estimated cost for running shoes: $50 to $150.

Calculating Your Total Triathlon Equipment Costs

Now that you have a general idea of how much this triathlon stuff will deplete your savings account, let's do some addition. Fill out the Equipment Cost Worksheet. You may already have some of this gear. If not, perhaps borrowing or buying used is an alternative for you.

Equipment Cost Worksheet

Item	Estimated cost	What you can afford
Racing swimsuit	$20-$80	
Swimming goggles	$10-$50	
Wetsuit	$100-$250	
Bicycle	$800-$1,200	
Bicycle accessories	$200-$400	
Running shoes	$50-$150	
Other:		
Other:		
	Total:	

Part II
Triathlon Training Basics

Not every newcomer to triathlon comes from a swimming, cycling, and running background. You may have some experience in one or two activities or perhaps no real competitive experience in any of the three. The following part applies to a varied group of triathletes, from the experienced endurance athlete to the aspiring weekend warrior. Each chapter contains a "Do's and Don'ts" section for those with little or no experience in each leg of the triathlon, but even you veteran swimmers, cyclists, or runners can find some of the training tips and workout schedules helpful.

Chapter 4

Swim Training:
The Key Is Technique

> "It's no secret that triathlons would be much larger if they didn't have that swim part."
>
> —*Terry Laughlin*

More than a decade ago, I found myself in a beginner's swim class at Daley College on the south side of Chicago. It was the middle of winter, and I was learning the front crawl in the hopes of completing a triathlon the following summer. I was starting from square one.

I was 23 years old, and I couldn't go one lap in a pool without gasping for air. I had a fear of water, especially deep water; this fear had been with me all my life. A near-drowning incident when I was 10 years old in a hotel pool during a family vacation had left an indelible imprint on me and was no doubt a contributing factor to my general ineptitude and anxiety in the pool.

But my ego and childhood fears aside, taking a swimming class was the right move to make. Little by little, drill by drill, I graduated from walking across the pool mimicking the front crawl stroke to actually stroking and sticking my head in the water at the same time. Later, I added the kick, and voila! I could swim a lap. Within a few months, I was swimming. I signed up for intermediate swimming and then advanced swimming with Coach Hajak, who helped me hone my skills for open water.

By the time triathlon season rolled around, I was a swimmer, albeit a slow one. I was the last out of the small lake in Bloomington, Illinois at my first triathlon 10 years ago (my open water navigational skills were not quite up to par—I zigzagged a lot).

My swim training was the most challenging aspect of training for my first triathlon, and I'll always consider learning to swim one of my greatest personal achievements. Not just because my learning to swim enabled me to finish my first triathlon, but because I managed to look in the eye a personal demon that had stared me down for 13 years.

The Water-Challenged

Take an informal survey of most triathletes, and I'm sure you'll find that my story is not unique. Although the fears, lessons learned, and experiences are different, a large percentage of triathletes find swimming to be the most challenging event.

In many ways, that's ironic. First, the swim is usually the event that takes up the least amount of total time, with cycling and running comprising the vast majority of a race. Second, swimming is generally less taxing on the body than cycling and running, particularly forgiving to leg muscles and knee joints. Third, unless open water conditions are unfavorable, the energy expended during a swim does not typically match the bike ride and the run (except for pros and other top age-group athletes competing for prize money or accolades).

So with all the good news about swimming, why is it such a big deal, especially to many first-time triathletes? There are probably as many answers to that question as there are triathletes. Suffice it to say that, for whatever personal reason, learning to swim and training properly may be your biggest obstacles.

Racing Tip

Sometimes getting yourself to relax about swimming is all a matter of attitude. Many triathletes look at the swim leg of a race as simply a "warm-up" to the hard part—the bike ride and run. You may find that hard to believe, but when you graduate to longer distances, you'll definitely find that to be true. Even if you're doing a sprint distance race, try thinking of the swim leg as a warm-up. Then maybe that quick dip won't seem so intimidating.

If You're New to Swimming: Do's and Don'ts

If you're just getting your feet wet in swimming, don't be intimidated. All it takes to learn how to swim is a little courage, self-discipline, and some good instruction. As with the next few training chapters, I'll provide some do's and don'ts for the first-timer:

• **Do take a beginner's swim class.** Do like I and many other triathletes have done—seek instruction at a local city college or adult-education course. The YMCA in your area might also offer swim classes. If you look hard enough, you'll find a beginner's class to get you started on many happy laps.

• **Don't recruit a friend as an instructor.** Don't make the common mistake of recruiting someone you know that you *think* may be a good swimmer (or who may *say* they are a good swimmer). Often times, those reputations or self-concepts are inflated, and rarely will you get good instruction this way. Your best bet, again, is to seek professional instruction from a swim coach that conducts a class.

• **Do stick with it.** As we'll discuss in a bit, swimming is more technical and skill-oriented than cycling and running. Therefore, learning to swim the front crawl properly involves learning a sequence of skills. These skills are often taught independently, and then combined gradually. Exhaling underwater, turning your head to breathe, stroking, kicking, maintaining good body position—acquiring all of these skills and more requires a methodical and sometimes painstaking process. Be patient and have faith in your instructor. Though the prescribed drills may seem mundane and wear on you mentally, practice them in the order they are given. You'll be glad you did later on.

• **Don't jump the gun.** There's nothing worse than feeling discouraged. A sure way to discourage yourself from learning to swim is to attempt a full-blown lap swimming workout when you've only taken one week of beginner's instruction. Again, swimming is a technical sport, and it takes time to perfect technique. Practice the drills, and worry about lap swimming later.

• **Do practice on your own.** A better way to use your energy than trying to lap swim too early is to set aside some time away from class to practice the drills learned in your last class. When I took beginner's swimming, I knew I wouldn't be ready in six months for my first triathlon if I just attended the twice-a-week classes without some extra effort. So I set aside three additional days during the week when the pool was open for practicing the drills I'd learned the previous class.

Also, when you are first learning a new activity, it's best to get in as much practice as close to the instruction as possible. That way you learn faster and retain more. If you're serious about learning to swim, set aside at least two or three sessions per week—even if they are short 15-minute sessions—for practicing the most recent lesson on your own.

• **Don't learn bad habits.** Although you may feel at a disadvantage if you are new to swimming, you are in the unique position of learning to swim the front crawl properly. Because technique plays a big role in swimming, bad habits abound. Just sit in on a masters group swim session at a local YMCA. You'll see arms flailing and slapping the water in every direction, horrendous flutter kicks that send spouts to the ceiling, and bad breathing habits that make you wonder whether there are enough lifeguards on deck. By being a newcomer, you can avoid bad habits that will slow you down with every yard you swim. Even if you aren't completely new to the front crawl, concentrate on letting go of any bad habits you have developed by learning technique via drills all over again.

Intervals and Those Darn Math Equations

Even if swim training is new to you, you may have heard of "interval" training or "repeats." This type of training is frequently used for cycling and run training as well. Intervals are simply multiple, short, moderate-to high-intensity bursts of effort over a measured distance, with some sort of recovery between each interval or repeat. The purpose is to get your body used to swimming (or cycling or running) at a faster pace, thereby improving technique and increasing endurance.

Maybe you've also seen those puzzling math equation-looking things on the blackboard next to the pool. The following figure shows a sample interval training notation, along with an explanation of what each number means.

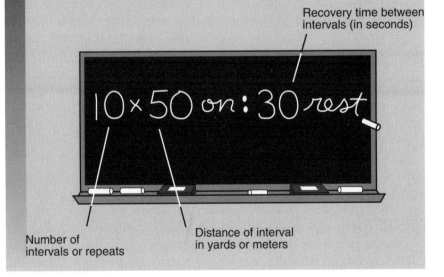

Recovery time between intervals (in seconds)

Number of intervals or repeats

Distance of interval in yards or meters

If You're Already a Swimmer

If you're entering the sport of triathlon from a swimming background, you've got a significant psychological advantage over many triathletes that dread the swim leg. Here's some tips you should keep in mind if you've got gills instead of lungs:

• **Focus on technique.** Even veteran swimmers need to continuously hone their efficiency in the water. If you've developed bad habits, such as a lazy stroke in one arm or a flutter kick that churns up water, now's the time to improve in those areas. Remember, you've got to bike and run after a swim, so the more efficient you are, the better off you'll be.

• **Learn open water skills.** This tip goes for everyone, but if your swim background comes primarily from pool swimming, then you need to experience open water. Dealing with waves and navigating a race course are skills that pool swimming doesn't teach you. (More on open water swimming later in this chapter.)

• **Become a land lover.** Don't spend all your training time in the pool. Swimming comprises the shortest portion of a triathlon, and you're presumably comfortable and proficient in water. Spend the majority of your training time cycling and running.

Going to Camp

Terry Laughlin is an expert swim coach and founder of Total Immersion Swim Camps. He is also an author and has put on swim clinics around the world. If you've been around triathlon for a while, there's no missing the Total Immersion way of swimming. Much of what I and countless other triathletes have learned about proper swim technique has been from Terry, either though the numerous articles he's authored for every major triathlon magazine, his videotape, book, or the swim camps he puts on throughout the nation.

I first attended his swim camp several years ago, going into the camp with a misconception about swimming I'd carried in my mind for a long time. Having a fairly trim and lanky build, I assumed that my lack of buoyancy put me at a natural disadvantage in swimming. I reasoned that, sure, I'd be able to compete in triathlons (with the aid of a wetsuit), but I would never be very fast in the water. As a result, I divided almost all my training time between running and cycling and hoped that backpack propeller motors would be sanctioned for racing.

With my running and cycling speeds peaking and my race times still unsatisfying, I decided to tackle the swimming issue head on and was fortunate enough to spot an ad in *Triathlete* for Total Immersion Adult Swim Camps. "You should be able to shave minutes off your 1.5 kilometer time after the three-day camp," said Terry as I requested an application over the phone. I was hopeful, but nonetheless skep-

Terry Laughlin's Total Immersion Swim Camps combine classroom and poolside instruction with drill practice.

tical. He told me that the camp focused on technique as opposed to conditioning, drills instead of workouts. Though I'd been a consistent practitioner of drills, I felt that my lack of buoyancy should be offset by developing upper body strength and stroke power.

"After this weekend, you'll realize that good swimming is not about buoyancy or body fat or upper body strength. It's about getting your body in the right position," said Laughlin during the orientation. "It's about balance." During that weekend, Laughlin taught me and the others at the camp some key principles of swim training that have helped me not only swim faster, but more efficiently and with less effort. The camp was a mix of classroom instruction and pool time, but a large portion of the weekend was spent drilling, and drilling, and drilling.

The first key principle Laughlin introduced us to was that of swimming balance. Using a partner in the pool deck, we took part in an exercise that showed us the proper balance position for swimming. The point, Laughlin stressed to us, was that with proper balance and keeping the head connected to the rest of the body, you'll stay horizontal in the water (as opposed to the familiar sagging lower body that I had accepted like unwanted baggage).

After some instruction on a pool drill to help establish balance, and with my partner watching me, I jumped into the pool to test the theory. To my amazement, my buttocks skimmed the surface of the water as I did a relaxed kick. I could feel it instantly. The experience was similar for most of the other participants, some showing obvious shock in their ability to stay horizontal in the water. "I thought that there was no hope for me," said 48-year-old Chicago triathlete Greg Jay Valent. "For the last two years, I've felt more tired while swimming, and I was getting slower, like I was fighting the water. I can already tell this will really help me."

"The biggest impact you can make in swimming is not by increasing your power," said Laughlin. "It's by eliminating resistance through balancing. In the water, you're moving against something that's 1,000 times more dense than air, so a horizontal position and staying balanced throughout each phase of the swimming stroke is crucial."

Toward the second half of camp, the second key principle Laughlin demonstrated was hip rotation and "swimming on your side." Through a series of classroom instructions and pool drills, the concept that greater arm extension and power came from rotating the hips was engraved in our minds. "The engine is not in the arms and shoulder, it's in the hip," said Laughlin. "If you look at the top swimmers, they don't have huge upper bodies. They don't power through the water. Great swimmers stay balanced and rotate their hips so that they use the least amount of energy necessary to accomplish the most."

By the second day of camp, I and many of the other triathletes began to accept that interval workouts and long swims were not the key to better swimming. Schooled in the "the more mileage, the better" mentality, I began to realize that swimming required an altogether different approach. "You have to look at swimming as a motor skill activity, like tennis, golf, or skiing," said Laughlin. "And look at conditioning as something that occurs as a result of practicing technique. Triathletes tend to have difficulty seeing this because most come from a running or cycling background."

Laughlin's swim drills are too lengthy to go into here in great detail. Besides, you'll learn them better from him than from a single chapter in a book (see the appendix for the Total Immersion phone number). But I did ask Terry to address the specific swim training information the beginner or newcomer to the sport needs to succeed. Toward the end of this chapter, he also briefly describes a few fundamental drills.

Open water swimming may seem intimidating, but proper technique can help you minimize any anxiety you may have.

Terry's Shrewd Tips for Your First Triathlon Swim

Nothing against the hundreds of experienced triathletes I've coached in Total Immersion workshops, mind you, but I've got news for everyone who might be thinking of tackling a triathlon. If you work the swim right, this sport is only two-thirds as tough as you think it is. For although there's no question that endurance counts—name another sport that calls a two-hour race a "sprint" with a straight face—the process of training for a triathlon needn't swallow you whole. You just need to know how to minimize the work that does you the least good.

Two Good Reasons to Relax

You'd never find the word "relax" in the gospel according to most triathletes, which says you simply train and train until you can keep moving for anywhere from 2 hours (sprint) to 16 hours (Ironman). Training usually means just one thing: mile upon mile of swimming, and running, and cycling.

At first glance that strategy may make sense, but looked at more critically, I believe there's strong evidence to suggest that time-consuming endurance training is far less helpful for swimming—and may even hurt your performance—than it is for biking and running. If I'm right, there may be solid reason to cut miles off the weekly training volume you thought you'd need for a creditable swim leg.

Reason one is that the swim comes first in a triathlon. In a sprint triathlon, most competitors are finished with the waterborne quarter-mile or half-mile in 20 minutes or less. But you may not be dismounting your bike until 90 or more tough minutes have ticked by, and a lot of new triathletes will still be out there on the running course two hours or more after they started their day's labors. When is a serious energy shortage most likely to develop? Right, later in the

Training error #23: Never block the swimming lanes with your stationary bicycle.

race. So cumulative fatigue—and the need to train yourself to resist it—is obviously much greater in running and biking than in swimming. On top of that, think of the limited work your swimming muscles do compared to your cycling and running muscles. The swim leg is always the shortest of the three, typically lasting just one-third to one-quarter as long as the run and bike legs.

The second reason to cut back on your swimming training time is that swimming, compared to running and biking, is fundamentally an unnatural activity in which practice—without coaching, at least—does not make perfect. In running or cycling, where mechanical efficiency is so much higher, more training mileage makes a positive difference; in the water, it's a waste of time and energy for most people. When you swim more and more miles, as you do in most tri-training programs, you're more likely to be practicing your mistakes than refining your technique and boosting your endurance. You're not becoming a more efficient swimmer; you're just getting better at swimming inefficiently.

Efficiency is what triathlon swimming is all about. It's not how fast you finish the wet "leg," it's how easily. You've got a lot of work ahead of you once you're back on land, and saving energy may be the most important thing you can do in the water to help your overall finishing time. Standing behind the starting line on race day, think of what you're about to do in the water after the gun goes off as simply a way of getting to the real race start, the bike. Triathlon swimming and triathlon swim training should be more about race management than about racing. So train like a manager, not like a machine. It's not how strong you are, it's how you use your strength.

Terry's Fish School:
Intelligent Triathlon Swim Training

Fish go farther, faster, on less energy than we'll ever manage. But we can borrow some of their most efficient techniques by using the nervous system, not the aerobic. This Total Immersion plan replaces simple yardage, repeats, and intervals with four strategies of fishlike swimming:

- **Count your strokes regularly.** Your best measure of efficiency is how many strokes you take getting from one end of the pool to the other. As fatigue mounts and efficiency falls, your stroke count can balloon by 30 percent or more as you diligently train your nervous system to lapse into inefficiency.

- **Practice stroke elimination.** Make efficiency, not yardage or speed, your objective. Set a stroke-count target of 10 percent lower than your norm. For example, if you usually take 22 strokes per length on endurance swims or repeats, set a new limit for yourself of just 20. See how far into a swim or set you can hold that count instead of how fast you can finish or how tight an interval you can manage.

- **Streamline yourself with skills.** Whenever you're not counting strokes, work on getting your nervous system used to efficiency-promoting skills that make you more "fishlike." None of these skills come naturally, and all take work to get used to, but they produce results. These three skills will make an immediate difference:

    1. **Get that head down.** Forget the old rule about looking forward and keeping the waterline at your forehead. That utterly unnatural position just tires you out and wrecks your "torpedo" shape. If more than a sliver of the back of your head shows above the surface as you swim, you're holding your head too high. Ask a friend to check you.

    2. **Swim downhill.** Shift your weight forward until you feel as if you're leaning on your chest. This shift keeps your body more horizontal, more "slippery," making your hips and legs feel lighter. That reduces the need to kick and tire out your leg muscles, for which they'll thank you later in the race.

    3. **Swim taller.** Say to yourself each stroke, "The most important thing I do with my hand is lengthen my body. Reach, reach, reach! Don't pull, pull, pull." That gives you a longer stroke and a longer, sleeker "vessel" that will slice far more easily through the water. Ask any naval architect. Remember to keep your head down and swim downhill or this may be impossible. Slice your hand in close to your head, instead of reaching over the water.

- **Swim less, drill more.** If, despite your best efforts, you find yourself unable to reduce your stroke count to a consistent 20 strokes per 25 yards, you're better off doing more drills and less swimming. Your stroke inefficiencies are so stubborn that every lap you do makes them more permanent. The only way to break those stubborn bad "human swimming" habits and build new fishlike ones is to spend more time doing drills than conventional swimming. Try doing at least 60 percent of your yardage in stroke drills for the next month or two and see how your stroke reacts. Even when you do reduce your stroke count to 20 strokes per 25 yards, drills should constitute at least 25 percent of your total workout time. Happy laps!

Terry's Tips on Overcoming the Open Water Willies

For many triathletes, it's not swimming that is feared, it is swimming in open water. Whether in a small lake, one of the Great Lakes, or the ocean, open water swimming can be a source of extreme anxiety for the first-time triathlete.

For Those Who Fear Taking the Plunge

Carol Zanoni turned up at one of my Total Immersion swim camps hoping to fulfill a dream. The Teaneck, New Jersey athlete runs a strong marathon and can bike like a seasoned racer too, but her first attempt at a triathlon ended in disappointment when she suffered a panic attack just a short distance into the swim leg and had to drop out. Her goal: learn to swim comfortably and competently in open water and make it to the bike leg.

How many other thousands of would-be triathletes, people who can run all day long and have perfectly good bikes in the garage, still shrink from their first race? It's that open water swim. Even those who may be able to cruise, gracefully or otherwise, from one end of the pool to the other recognize that swimming without a line to guide you, a bottom you can see, and a wall nearby for comfort is a whole other story. Buoys to find, surf (and other competitors) to fight, and who knows what else is in the water out there. Who needs it?

Then there are those who aren't afraid of open water; they just can't swim very well in it. I can't count the number of triathletes who showed up at one of my camps this year saying, "Just once I'd like to come up to the beach and see some other bikes besides mine in the transition area."

I've offered both types the same advice. Although your success in the bike ride or run is primarily a measure of how well you've trained, success in the swim leg depends mainly on how well you've practiced. Adopt a new philosophy for the pool: Conditioning is something that happens to you while you're practicing technique and pacing skills.

If you can swim for 30 minutes nonstop in the pool without feeling wiped out, there's no reason you can't handle the open water swim leg of a triathlon without too much hassle. Success in the swim leg involves two steps: intelligent preparation in the pool and strategic rehearsal in open water. Neither one's a "workout;" both are "practice."

Practice in the Pool

There are a number of ways to prepare for open water swimming in a pool. In my swim camps, I teach a variety of different drills and activities, each designed to achieve an objective that can help you swim in open water better. It's impossible for me to teach these lessons to you here; it takes much more time and effort. But at the very least, you should be aware that you can learn a number of tangible skills and techniques to make open water much less nerve-racking.

These drills and activities include the following:

- Stroke drills to learn greater stroke efficiency by practicing the three fishlike skills described on page 67–68
- Sensory swimming, which focuses on one specific sensation (such as feeling balanced)
- Stroke eliminator swims to test your stroke efficiency
- Longer swims using greater stroke efficiency for consistency

Practice in Open Water

Before the race, do some swimming in a lake or the ocean. It'll get you used to the absence of convenient guides like lane lines. You'll learn to navigate using on-shore landmarks. For safety's sake, swim with an experienced partner or a group, or with a canoe or kayak escort, or in water you know very well. In cold water, stay close to shore. Hypothermia (lowered body temperature) can compromise your coordination and judgment. Wear a wetsuit if the water makes you feel very chilled.

Don't just swim; practice the same technical points you've been practicing in the pool. The idea is to give yourself an orderly transition from your pool practice to an open water race, so make it an open water practice. Swim downhill, reach forward with a weightless arm, roll your hips from side to side, and so on. You can't count laps out here? No problem. Count strokes instead. Practice a technique for 100 strokes or more. Not having walls actually makes it easier. Your rhythm isn't interrupted, and you'll find it's easier to "groove" your stroke.

Some Fundamental Swim Drills

Here are the first few swim drills that I teach in my Total Immersion workshops. My drills are designed to teach skills in progression, with one drill laying the foundation for the next. Thus these few drills provide only a glimpse of the fundamentals needed for "fishlike" swimming.

Pressing the Buoy

This drill teaches you how to find the right head position and amount of buoy pressure to balance your body. Start with your head in the anatomical position (the position that you normally hold it in when you're not in the water). Push off with your head in the water looking down. Kick with a small gentle flutter, arms lightly hugging your sides. Press your buoy (chest area) gently into the water until your buttocks barely break the surface of the water (see below). You should feel as though the water is supporting more of your body weight, which will likely help you to relax. Lift your head to breathe when you need to, but try and re-establish balance quickly.

Side Balancing

This drill introduces the most critical position for balance. Kick on one side of your body with your lower shoulder touching your chin. Lean on your lower shoulder as you look at the pool bottom (see next page). This may be difficult to do, so start out with short distances (6 to 10 yards) to master balance in this position. Repeat with the opposite side. When you feel you've mastered this, try kicking on your side the length of the pool, swiveling your head upward when you need to breathe. Swim back on your opposite side.

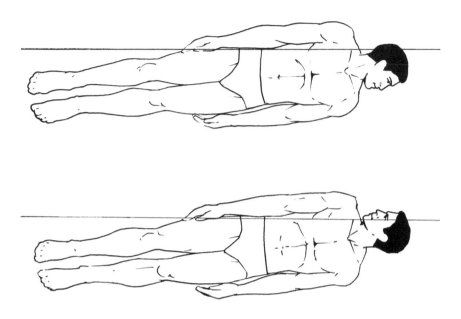

Balance on Your Back

This exercise lays the groundwork for further drills that help you to achieve balance in every phase of your stroke. Kick easily on your back, hands at your sides, shoulders slightly rounded, and chin slightly tucked. Press your buoy (which, when you're on your back, is the back of your head and your upper spine) to keep your hips up. Feel your hips and thighs move closer to the surface as you press. Knees and toes should be just under the surface, but should not break through (see below). Practice short distances until your balance feels natural and easy.

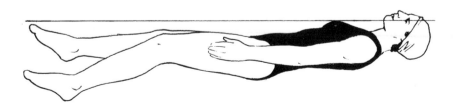

Persistence, Determination, and a Pull Buoy

Diane Berberian's first triathlon was every beginner's nightmare. Without any open water experience, she stood on the beach before the start of the large, high-profile 1989 St. Anthony's Triathlon and looked out over the rough water. Minutes later, she found herself getting tossed around in the choppy waves, her competitors speeding away from her. Feeling alone and in danger, she panicked and quickly began to hyperventilate. Fortunately, lifeguards were there and pulled her out of the water. "I was totally discouraged," says the 39-year-old St. Petersburg resident. "I went home and I cried for three hours. I swore that I would never be a triathlete because I did not know how to swim."

After her open water scare, she took a five-year hiatus from triathlon, choosing instead to concentrate on duathlons, road races, and marathons. But many of her friends were triathletes, and she envied all the fun they seemed to be having. At the end of 1993, she attended a party to watch the broadcast of the Ironman Triathlon in Hawaii. Inspired, she went home and mapped out her training schedule. Days later, she hired a swim coach to give her lessons and was in the pool practicing every day for months. When she felt ready to try open water again, she practiced with a friend on each side of her, swimming in calm waters. To help her feel even safer, she swam with a pull buoy.

Months later, she stood on the beach of the 1994 Clermont Sprint Race, a small, local race with a friendly atmosphere. As a result of all her hard work, she was more confident in her swimming, more comfortable in open water, and much better prepared. "I felt relatively safe and comfortable, a much different experience than my first attempt. Most importantly, I had fun," says Diane of her completed swim leg that day, which she successfully followed with her first triathlon finish. Since then, she has completed more than 30 races, including an Ironman-distance race in Florida and the prestigious Ironman Triathlon in Hawaii.

Chapter 5

Bike Training: Putting in the Mileage

> "The will to win is nothing without the will to prepare."
>
> —*Juna Ikunga*

It's often said that triathlons all come down to the run. I disagree. Although you certainly have to be a good runner to be competitive in triathlon, you first have to come off the bike with legs that haven't been mangled beyond their running abilities.

A good example of this is my rivalry with my friend, Guillermo. A few years ago when we competed against each other regularly, Guillermo was a much better runner than I. From 5K road races to marathons, the longer the race, the farther behind I finished. When we both entered the world of multisport, I took to cycling with as much enthusiasm and energy as I had done with marathoning. Guillermo, on the other hand, avoided putting in miles on the bike. He was nervous about riding on roads, even low-traffic ones, and never quite got the hang of dealing with the close proximity of other cyclists in group rides.

As a result, my cycling ability was greater than his, although I could run no faster. Because we were both of equal swimming ability, I assumed that our cycling and running times would offset each other, and that we'd finish any triathlon at about the same time. Much to my surprise, I was maintaining my lead off the bike and consistently crossing the finish line well ahead of him. What had changed? My run times were about average, if not slower than usual, so I knew I wasn't running any faster.

In reviewing the race results, it became obvious that Guillermo had slowed on the run because the cycling had beaten him up so much. Without the proper training and necessary cycling mileage under his belt, he would start the run on achy, sore, tired legs, sometimes coming close to cramping. It didn't matter that he had a better runner's body than I, or that his marathon best beat mine by more than 30 minutes. By not properly training on the bike, he had effectively negated his natural running ability.

The lesson to be learned: although most triathlons finish with a run, it doesn't matter how good a runner you are if you don't have legs left off the bike. So what if you're not interested in competing, but just hoping to finish your first triathlon? The same lesson applies.

Cycling: The Core of Triathlon

Because many triathletes come from a running background, cycling is often the second most feared event of the three. Although cycling is usually not as intimidating as open water swimming to the newcomer, there are many reasons some triathletes avoid two-wheel training. Some find the speeds too nerve-racking, or perhaps the danger of riding in traffic is a factor. Others simply find cycling uncomfortable or monotonous.

No matter what the aversion (if you have one) to cycling, there's no getting around the fact that riding comprises the majority of time in a triathlon. Yep, no matter what distance you train for, you'll spend most of it on a bicycle saddle. So if you're not used to the idea of doing some riding, now is a good time to get used to it.

That's not to say you may find the experience of putting in some miles on the bike unpleasant. You may very well find the open roads to be an escape from everyday stress, group rides to be great social outings, and the dizzying speeds of downhills to be peak experiences.

Cycling comprises the majority of a triathlon so learn to love the open roads.

If You're New to Cycling: Do's and Don'ts

Although almost everybody has done some recreational cycling, organized or competitive riding may be new to you. The rules of the road are still the same (although many recreational cyclists don't follow them), but the penalty for breaking them can be a severe accident. Here are some do's and don'ts for those of you who haven't ridden your Schwinn since you were knee-high:

• **Do ride with traffic.** Kevin Bacon may get his kicks running head on into cars as a bike messenger (remember the movie *Quicksilver*?), but your best chance of staying alive in traffic is to follow the rules of the road. Contrary to what you may see in busy downtown streets, the proper (and legal) way to ride on roadways is with traffic, not against. Another common error is weaving in between parked cars, which makes it difficult for motorists to see you until it's too late. Ride in a straight line, avoid erratic or sudden turns, and ride defensively.

• **Don't ride on busy streets or paths.** It amazes me when I see serious cyclists riding on busy roadways, with hundreds of cars whizzing by them within inches of their limbs. Not everybody has the good fortune to live near rural roads; living in large cities makes it doubly difficult to find open roads for cycling. But thousands of bicyclists are hit, sometimes fatally, by cars on highly trafficked roadways. If you don't live near rural roadways with low traffic, get yourself a bike rack and drive to a location that has safer training routes. Yes, it's a pain and takes more time from your busy schedule, but your ride will be much more enjoyable and, best of all, safer. Another helpful tip: if you can arrange to ride during a time of day when there may be less traffic on the roadways, all the better.

• **Do participate in group and organized rides.** Bicycle clubs and shops in virtually every well-populated area of the country sponsor weekly rides, and longer organized rides take place almost every weekend. Organized rides are an ideal way to train, providing you with an opportunity to mix with a group of men and women who are near your current riding ability. Most large groups consist of a wide range of riding talent, from the slowpoke talkers to the stone-faced quad machines. Weekend century rides with frequent food stops range from 20 to 100 miles; they are excellent opportunities to get in a good chunk of mileage without having to worry about carrying enough fluids and food with you. These events also help with the mental obstacle—the boredom that can set in when doing distances over 25 miles.

- **Don't ride an uncomfortable bike.** I've already talked about how important it is to get a properly fitted bicycle, but this point can't be stressed enough. Nobody likes to be uncomfortable in an activity that may last an hour or longer, and riding a bicycle that doesn't fit or detracts from your comfort in any way is just no fun. Other factors that affect comfort are the choice of a bicycle saddle (no real rule of thumb here—you just have to keep trying them until you find one that fits your unique butt) and padded bicycle shorts.

- **Do be ready for anything.** Unlike swimming in a pool at the YMCA or running within a few miles from your doorstep, cycling can take you some formidable distances. You may find yourself 10 or more miles from home, perhaps on some country road without a soul in sight. So it's very important to ensure that you are ready for any kind of mishap, mechanical or otherwise, that may occur out there.

First and foremost, never ride without a bicycle helmet. Be sure you know how to fix a flat; have a friend or your local bicycle shop show you. Always carry at least two tubes and a pump (or CO_2 air cartridges) with you at all times. Even if you're not mechanically inclined, carry a multipurpose cycling tool that will fit in a behind-the-saddle frame bag for simple repairs. Always carry a credit card, driver's license, and cash. For longer rides on rural roads, a cellular phone is a pretty good idea.

- **Don't be intimidated.** Newcomers to the sport may find cycling intimidating for a couple of reasons. First, the expensive tri-bicycles you're sure to find in the transition area of any competitive triathlon (particularly hotly contested, large events such as Ironman qualifying races) are enough to make anybody rolling in with a mountain bike or old clunker feel a little bit ashamed. Don't be. As discussed in chapter 3, there's no need for you to spend a ton of money on bicycle stuff at the onset, especially if you're just beginning in the sport and aren't interested in competing. Roll in that clunky, but trusty, steed of yours in the transition area with pride!

Second, if you happen to begin to ride with road racers, not triathletes, who are dedicated solely and seriously to cycling, you may find their approach a little more intense. As you'll find in chapter 7, triathlon training and training in individual sports are two very

Suddenly, Melvin sensed BIG competition.

different approaches. Don't be alarmed or put off from cycling because of your exposure to "roadies." No matter what type of competitive cycling (criteriums, time trials, road races, track racing) these serious cyclists are training for, their methods of training will be different.

If You're Already a Cyclist

Although the veteran swimmer has the psychological edge over those who dread water, the seasoned cyclist entering multisports has a physical advantage over anybody with little cycling experience. Here's some things to keep in mind if your quads have their own zip code:

- **Get used to riding alone.** If you come from a road racing background, then you may have gotten quite good at drafting and comfortably riding in a paceline. (More on drafting later for those not familiar with the term.) However, triathlons are more like time trials than road races, so adjust your training accordingly. You can still do the occasional pro bike shop ride or road race for fun and competition, but make sure the majority of your training is done without drafting.

- **Get over any aversion to aero bars.** It took the road racing community a long time to accept aero bars, and some traditionalists still scoff at their use, even for time trialing (although they are now in the minority). Put simply, aero bars provide a significant performance advantage, and my guess is that, as a veteran cyclist, you want to do well on the bike leg of a race. Aero bars will help you do that (more on aerodynamics and aero bars later in this chapter).

- **Get in the pool and pound the pavement.** The temptation may be to focus on becoming a better cyclist, but your efforts are better spent focusing on your weaknesses, not your strength. Cycling will comprise the majority of time in any proper triathlon training program, but that doesn't give you license to skip the other two sports. One tip: cycling is a great sport because of the camaraderie, so join master swimming groups and group runs to help get you motivated for those activities.

Spinning Your Way to Success

Even if you can't quote the gear ratios on your bicycle (I can't either), you're probably somewhat familiar with your bike's multiple gears. These gears allow you to change resistance to accommodate your current ability level and varying terrain, such as uphills and downhills. You're no doubt aware that some gears are very easy to pedal, and others send your quadriceps into overload.

Learning to use gearing to accommodate workout goals and handle varying terrain effectively is a skill that you gradually acquire by experimentation and practice. Little by little, mile by mile, you'll learn which gear you feel most comfortable in—the one that doesn't feel too hard or too easy for the moment. Your inclination may be to find the biggest possible gear to mash. Until your legs (particularly your knees) adapt to the cycling motion and you are confident that your cycling ability has reached a competitive level where speedwork becomes a viable training technique, however, hammering big gears will do you more harm than good.

What exactly is spinning? Spinning is pedaling at high RPMs (revolutions per minute) to help increase efficiency. More importantly for the beginner, spinning is a safe way to avoid knee injury, learn correct pedaling technique, and adapt to the unique motion of cycling. Most experts contend that pedaling at 85 to 95 RPMs is a good spinning range. How do you know your RPMs? The best way is to purchase a computer with a cadence feature, which displays your RPMs at the push of a button. Without a computer with cadence, it's difficult to tell if you are spinning, especially for a novice cyclist.

In general, the resistance when you are spinning should feel relatively easy, but not so soft and rapid that your pedaling motion becomes choppy, erratic, or out of control. Pedaling should feel smooth, and your focus should be on completing the entire 360-degree pedal stroke efficiently, without any "dead spots" or bursts of power. Each pedal stroke should feel controlled and tight all the way around. If you train in a hilly area, it's more difficult to spin throughout an entire workout. Use your entire range of gears, and don't be afraid to use your easiest gear (largest cog and your smallest chain ring) to maintain high RPMs on uphills.

Although we'll go into specific training workouts and recommendations in chapter 7, it's important to note here that spinning should comprise the first few hundred miles of cycling. In fact, for shorter or middle-distance triathlons, spinning may be your entire training method.

The Drafting Thing

Unlike the swim leg of a triathlon where you'll often be an arm's length away from a fellow competitor, cycling rules prohibit close proximity to other riders. Why is that? Simply put, the triathlon is designed to be based on individual effort, and sometimes riding close to another cyclist provides a teamwork and performance advantage called drafting.

Drafting is a term that is used to describe riding in another cyclist's slipstream, which makes it easier to cut through the wind. Although drafting usually occurs when a rider rides closely behind another cyclist, you can also draft by riding behind and to either side of a cyclist. (This is why USA Triathlon prohibits amateur triathletes from riding within a range that covers the entire circumference of another rider.)

In order to understand why drafting is not allowed, it is important to comprehend the significant performance advantage it allows. The best way to do that is to try drafting with a training partner. When you are confident you are both heading into a strong headwind on an open, straight stretch of road, ride behind your friend's rear wheel. Instruct your friend not to make any sudden turns or brake (unless in an emergency).

If this is your first time drafting, don't get too close. One foot is fine. Although experienced road racers who thrive on using this technique get within an inch or less of another rider's wheel, it's best to play it safe and stay at a relatively safe distance. Don't get in your aero bar position. Place your hands on your brake hoods or on your brake levers, just in case. Keep your vision focused on what's ahead on the road so you will always be aware of any forthcoming hazards.

You will feel an immediate difference; wind resistance will be cut down dramatically. Considering that wind is your primary foe on the bike, drafting is a big deal. Depending on the direction of the wind and the proximity and location of your wheel to the lead cyclist, your effort level can decrease by anywhere from 10 to 40 percent while you are maintaining or even increasing your speed.

Drafting and Racing

Obviously, drafting goes against the basic principle of competing in triathlons, which is to test your individual endurance. For this reason, drafting is not allowed. However, you may have heard of certain drafting-sanctioned races. This fairly new development is strictly limited to the professionals competing in races put on by the world governing body of triathlon, called the International Triathlon Union (ITU). The thinking is that drafting-sanctioned races are more

Racing Tip

If you do enough racing, sooner or later you may be victimized by a fellow competitor who has decided to take the easy way out and ride your wheel. Although you may not be voluntarily aiding this person, USA Triathlon officials can disqualify all riders in a drafting situation, regardless of who is drafting who. To avoid this penalty, be aware of other competitors around you. If somebody tries drafting you, tell him or her to back off. If that doesn't work, pull off to the side and let the little weasel face the wind without your help.

exciting to watch. Thus the ITU has pushed the rule change to garner more publicity and Olympic inclusion. It's highly unlikely, however, that drafting will ever be allowed amongst the rank and file of triathletes. It would be far too dangerous.

Drafting as a Training Tool

Most triathletes choose not to draft during training rides because the best way to train for time-trial cycling is to become accustomed to the aero position and solo riding without the aid of a slipstream. However, in certain situations, drafting can be useful. For example, during group rides where packs form or a paceline is organized (a paceline is a line of cyclists taking turns breaking the wind on a rotating basis), participation depends on drafting. There's nothing wrong with training this way, providing it doesn't comprise the majority of your riding.

Also, when riding with a training partner of superior riding ability to yours, drafting can help you stay with him or her and put in more miles than you might be able to do by yourself. Your partner should agree and know that you are drafting, so he or she doesn't turn or brake suddenly.

Lastly, when done with a dependable partner, drafting can help you concentrate on your pedaling form and efficiency. With the wind at bay, spinning in a slipstream can help you focus on completing a full-circle pedaling motion. One note: unless it's otherwise agreed upon, drafting etiquette dictates that riders take brief turns breaking the wind. To put it more eloquently, don't "suck wheel" without "breaking a little wind" yourself.

Training Technique Basics

The kind of cycling you'll be doing for triathlons, known as time trialing, primarily requires endurance. Although cycling is not as technical as swimming, there are some important technical considerations for the beginner or newcomer to the sport.

Learn Bike-Handling Skills

If you frequent pro cycling shops or hang around USCF (United States Cycling Federation) bicycle racers, you may find that triathletes get a bad rap. In some ways, it's undeserved. After all, triathletes have been responsible for a myriad of cycling innovations that have brought new life into the sport. Innovations such as aero bars, aerodynamic wheels, super lightweight cranksets, stems, and other replacement parts have all come about or been popularized as a direct result of triathlon. Heck, they should be glad we came along.

Yet, in one respect, we triathletes deserve a little ribbing from our cycling brethren—we just aren't as good at handling our bikes. Time trialing (riding all by yourself from point A to point B) requires very little bike-handling skill. If you can pedal, make a turn, and hit your brakes, you can complete a ride. But just because good bike-handling skills aren't a necessity, doesn't mean you should avoid learning them. The ability to handle your bicycle in a variety of situations, some of them emergencies, can save your life or, at the very least, prevent a serious case of "road rash." Also, these skills will give you a sense of mastery of your bicycle, giving you more confidence to train effectively.

Many fundamental bike-handling skills will come naturally when you start putting in some miles. Another good way to learn these skills is to ride with more experienced cyclists and do what they do. If you don't know any experienced riders, seek instruction from your local cycling shop. Some of the most important skills to learn for safe cycling are cornering, braking, emergency braking, and hill climbing.

Getting Aero

When the "safety bicycle" was invented in 1885 by English bicycle manufacturer J.K. Starley, little thought went into aerodynamics. The focus then was on creating a functional frame for two wheels of equal diameter. Most conventional bicycle frames today are a derivative of the old-fashioned diamond geometry invented over 110 years ago.

Fortunately, today we know a lot more about aerodynamics. Even if you intend to finish your first triathlon cycling leg in an upright position on your granddaddy's bomber, you might be interested to know just how important aerodynamics can be, just in case you decide to give this triathlon stuff a more serious go.

Aerodynamics 101

To understand the importance of the aero bar and good aerodynamics, let's take a look at the four basic ways air moves around you on a bicycle:

- Air moves over the top of your head.
- Air moves around your right side.
- Air moves around your left side.
- Air moves around the bicycle frame, between your legs, and under and behind you.

In three out of these four categories, you can help yourself slip through the air better. Three things can reduce the drag caused by air traveling over your top and around your sides:

- A proper aero position
- An aerodynamic helmet
- Aero bars

Find the Aero Fit

What exactly is a proper aerodynamic position? It's a matter of controversy. However, one thing that all experts agree on is the importance of comfort. Without comfort, no matter how aerodynamic the position, you're not likely to stay in it.

"The best way to know if you've been set up correctly for the aero position is to look at pictures of the pros in triathlon magazines. If you look like they do, you're probably set up right.

Another good way to find your ideal aero position is to have the good people at your local pro bicycle shop take a look at you on aero bars. They can look for any adjustments that may improve your comfort level or aerodynamics. They may also use some instruments that measure your position relative to the stem, crankarm, and other "landmarks" on your bike that help them find the proper seat position for you. Even minor changes, such as a slightly more forward seat position, can help alleviate stress on your arms or give you greater pedaling extension power.

For example, a seat position that's too high will cause your hips to swivel at the 6 o'clock position of each pedal stroke, which may lead to soreness in your hips or, worse, a lower back injury. On the other hand, if your seat is too low, your knees will bear the brunt of all that downward pressure, which may send you scurrying to the sports doc. A seat that's too far forward or too far back can also make your knees sore, as well as your neck, shoulders, and back. Take a look at the pro triathlete on page 85 for an example of a good riding position.

Handling the Roads

Although there are plenty of unnerving things about getting into competitive cycling, such as high-speed downhills or riding in a pack, Marti Hobbs's biggest fear was pedals. After her winter purchase of an entry-level racing bike with clipless pedals, Marti realized she didn't feel comfortable attaching her feet to anything she couldn't simply lift her foot off of whenever she needed. Veteran cyclists know that clipless pedals are virtually just as easy to exit as conventional ones, requiring a simple twisting motion to detach oneself. Nevertheless, Marti needed to feel comfortable with the concept, so she set up her bike on an indoor windtrainer and practiced attaching and detaching herself to the clipless pedals.

"When I finally started riding outside in the spring," says the 39-year-old resident of Birmingham, Alabama, "I felt okay being attached to the pedals. It might sound silly, but I needed to feel comfortable with it before I got on the roads. It also took me awhile to learn bike-handling skills, which I'm still doing."

Marti's triathlon friends guided her through some of the major handling skills necessary to stay vertical on the bike. They taught her to shift body weight into a fast turn, position her pedals at the 12 o'clock position on the cornering side, and put her hands in just the right place on the handlebars. "I'm still getting used to riding," says Marti, who completed her first triathlon, a sprint distance race, in early 1997. "Now I'm more confident and more relaxed on the bike, which really makes training and racing a lot more fun."

Types of Cycling Training

As with running, there is a wide variety of cycling workouts to choose from. Chapter 7 covers workout planning, but the following is an overview of some typical workouts. If you are a beginner, some of these workouts, such as long rides, road races, and hill or power workouts, are not advisable until you get more experienced.

• **Building block rides.** These very short rides increase endurance and accustom the beginner to extended periods of time on the saddle. Do them at a relatively easy pace, preferably spinning. These rides should start at 5 miles and gradually increase to 10 or 15 miles. Saddle soreness is a very common symptom—don't worry; the muscles in your buttocks will harden, and the pain will eventually go away.

• **Medium-distance rides.** These rides are most useful for those training for an Olympic distance race (40K cycling leg). They can range from 20 to 30 miles, and the intensity depends on the race goal.

• **Long rides.** These rides are typically performed at a slow, even, conversational pace. They can range from 40 to 100 miles or more. The goal with long rides is primarily to increase endurance.

• **Recovery workouts.** These workouts are short rides at a low intensity, with a lot of spinning. They can range from 5 to 20 miles. The goal in these workouts is to recover from a difficult or long workout, such as a long run or ride. Spinning during recovery workouts helps to loosen up legs and alleviate soreness or fatigue.

• **Time trials.** Do these race simulation rides on a course with little or no stops and at an intensity that is close to or at your desired race pace. They are typically half of what the actual race distance is.

• **Group rides.** The intensity of these rides depends on the group. Most group rides go 25 to 40 miles. These rides can be killer workouts, great social gatherings, or a little bit of both.

• **Road races.** Many road races are USCF-sanctioned and therefore require a membership license. However, some races have a "Citizens" category for non-USCF members. You can participate in USCF 40K individual time trials, which are ideal race simulation workouts. Or you can try a road race, which can range from 20 to 50 miles or more, but road races will test your bike-handling skills, so don't attempt them until you are confident you can ride in a pack.

• **Hill or power workouts.** If you are fortunate (or unfortunate) enough to have some hilly terrain where you live, hill climbing can help you increase your strength and power, which are two components that will help you go faster. If not, you can accomplish similar results with power workouts, which integrate sprinting intervals in

A good aero position can save significant time on the bike.

the middle of a ride. One warning: these workouts are considered speedwork, and they should not be attempted without first completing the base training discussed in chapter 7.

Cycling Advice From a Pro

If you've ever been to some of the larger races that offer prize money to professional triathletes, you may have run into Lauren Jensen. How can you tell her apart from the two dozen other female triathletes at competitive events? That's easy. Just look for the female pro with the rubber shark attached to the top of her bike helmet.

"I started wearing the shark helmet at the '91 Ironman Triathlon Championship in Hawaii," says Lauren. "I wore it because I wanted

Why Do Male Triathletes Shave Their Legs?

That is perhaps one of the most frequently asked questions by newcomers to the sport. Competitive cyclists have been shaving their legs for many years, primarily because it reduces the vulnerability to infection from road rash, which is a scraping away of a layer of skin from a fall off the bike (a fairly common occurrence among pack-riding cyclists). Hairless legs also make care and treatment of road rash much easier and less painful.

Triathletes shave for the same reason, although road rash is not as common due to the less hazardous nature of time trialing. There are several other reasons male triathletes choose to shed their leg hair:

- It's easier to massage your legs or have a therapist work on them without hair.

- You can get in and out of a wetsuit faster.

- It's easier for your body to be marked with your race number before a triathlon.

- Some triathletes feel that it helps keep their legs cooler during a hot run.

- You can show off your fabulous triathlete legs.

to remind myself that the most important thing for me on that day was to have fun. I've worn it at every race since then."

Having "Jaws" riding with her isn't Lauren's only claim to fame. Since she turned professional in 1993, Lauren has won many of the top races in the country, including three victories at the all-women's Danskin Triathlon national series and three first place finishes at the Springfield Ironhorse Triathlon, a very competitive half-Ironman distance event. Lauren considers cycling to be her strength. Because she is a longtime coach to many beginning triathletes (including her mom), and author of several magazine articles about triathlon, I've asked her to provide some motivation to take with you on the road, as well as a few practical tips for triathlon bike training and racing.

The "Shark" on Taking a Bite out of Fear

In coaching triathletes new to the sport, I find that there's always an element of fear in their thinking. It's normal to have some fear of the

Professional triathlete Lauren Jensen in her famous shark helmet . . . just when you thought it was safe to get on your bike.

unknown, and for many of us, a triathlon can present a whole bag of unknowns. Those who fear speed, accidents, or mechanical breakdown may think of the cycling leg of a triathlon as particularly scary.

Others fear dropping out, finishing last, or looking foolish. Unfortunately, this fear is what keeps many from attempting a triathlon. However, those who do make it to the starting line find that once the gun goes off, triathlons are not as overwhelming as they thought.

The right cycling training should go a long way to helping alleviate many of your fears of finishing, because the bicycle leg comprises a majority of the miles you'll cover in a race. As for finishing last, the odds are against it. But even if you do finish last, you are ahead of everyone who didn't even "tri". Always keep in mind that triathlon training is a learning experience, and you'll gain confidence with each race. After racing for 10 years, I am still constantly learning things that make my racing faster and more enjoyable.

Lauren's Cycling Tips

I have several suggestions that may help your cycling training and racing to be more successful. Some of these ideas may be common sense to you, yet all of these tips come from mistakes I have made or have seen others make.

• **Use your gears wisely.** Don't push a gear that's too hard and wears down your legs (remember, you've got a run to do). Keep your cadence up around 90 RPMs. Anticipate what gear you will need to be in for any hills and shift early so you don't have to grind up the hill.

• **Practice using new equipment.** Don't enter a race with new bike parts that you haven't tested and mastered beforehand. This applies to aero bars, clipless pedals, saddles, wheels—just about anything on your bike that may adversely affect your riding. This advice is especially important for clipless pedals; make sure you can stop and dismount safely before using them in a race.

• **Practice U-turns.** Why a U-turn? Many races with out-and-back bike courses have a U-turn turnaround where you have to navigate around an orange cone. Many triathletes, even experienced ones, have found themselves kissing the road at these turnarounds. Find a safe place to practice sharp corners and U-turns that you might find on a race course. As in a race, always take them slowly.

• **Hydrate on the bike.** Many beginners wait until the run to start drinking fluids. That's a big mistake. You should be on a full tank of gas as you start the run, so don't forget to drink up on the bike.

• **Wear a helmet.** Helmets are required during races, but don't skip wearing one during your training. A helmet saved my life once. Even veteran cyclists can crash through no fault of their own. Don't be foolish and assume that you'll be safe without a helmet.

• **Keep your bike in good shape.** The two most common mistakes novice cyclists make are not keeping their bike chain lubricated and not keeping tires at the proper pressure. Buy lubricating oil and ask your bike shop owner about its proper usage. While you're there, buy a floor pump with a built-in pressure gauge.

• **Take a lighthearted approach.** I've got a rubber fin on my bike helmet to remind me what triathlon is all about: fun. If you need to be reminded of this when your training and racing get too serious, you can find rubber sharks in the toy department.

Chapter 6

Run Training:
Putting One Foot
in Front of the Other

> "Once you've run long enough to experience the stimulating effects of endurance exercise, it's hard to turn back."
>
> —*Jeff Galloway*

Ninety miles south of Phoenix lives a small tribe of native Mexican Indians with amazing running skills called the Tarahumaras. From birth to death, they run and run and run without pain or discomfort. They are known to chase down deer and horses and run anywhere from 40 to 150 miles in one day! Locals there often tell a joke that attests to the extraordinary running skill of the Tarahumaras: A tourist who was driving by a running Tarahumara stopped and asked if he would like a lift. The Tarahumara replied, "No, thanks. I'm in a hurry."

A group of researchers recently asked a group of Tarahumaras to run 26.2 miles to test their heart rate and blood pressure. (The Tarahumaras agreed, but found it amusing that they would want them to run *only* 26.2 miles.) The results were unbelievable: pulse rates averaged about 130 beats per minute, and blood pressure readings, which were low at the start, were even lower at the end of the staged marathon.

So what does this tell us about running and triathlon? First, it demonstrates that the potential for running performance and endurance is much greater than scientists are willing to admit and that most of us (except these native Mexicans) can imagine. Second, it could be argued that the Tarahumaras are an example of the potential of triathlon. After all, they usually don't run just once a day; they perform a variety of day-to-day activities, transitioning into running as the need arises. Most of all, the Tarahumaras are a shining example of the potential within all of us to achieve physical acts we may have previously thought unachievable.

Having Something Left

Whether you come from a running background or are new to the sport, the last leg of a triathlon can be the most demanding, both physically and mentally. You or I may not have the running gifts of the Tarahumaras, but there are training techniques and workouts that will help you avoid a death march at the end of a race.

Perhaps the best way to avoid the tired triathlon shuffle is not a running training technique at all, but rather proper pacing through the swim and the bike ride. Setting a maniacal pace through the swim and the bike ride is a common mistake of the first-time triathlete, especially one who has attained a certain degree of competency (and arrogance) with swimming and biking (keep this in mind for your next triathlon goal).

Proper race pacing aside, training for a good triathlon run leg means following many of the same principles veteran runners have followed for years. If you're a runner making inroads into multisports, that doesn't mean that your triathlon run schedule for a sprint

Workouts in Hell #464: Treadmills.

distance race should be identical to your 5K training. Like anything in life, it's not that simple. There are a few twists and turns and some new ways of training, and you may need give up a little more mileage than you might care to sacrifice for other activities—swimming and biking, for example.

Admittedly, of the three activities that comprise triathlon, multisport running bears the closest resemblance to its individual sport sibling. The main differences are not so much about running itself, but how it fits into the bigger picture of triathlon.

If You're New to Running: Do's and Don'ts

As in all sports, there is a right way and a wrong way to do things in running. Unfortunately, many non-runners just beginning multisports lack knowledge of the basics and, as a result, run themselves into a brick wall. If you're new to running, one of the first things you need to do is learn the fundamentals, from equipment to training to safety concerns. So let's take a look at some beginner's do's and don'ts:

• **Do run in good running shoes.** It may sound *too* basic, but you've probably seen it before, most often at the health clubs: Novice runners wearing basketball high-tops circling the one-hundredth-of-a-mile indoor running track. (Which is another mistake: never run on a track smaller than your bedroom.)

Become an educated consumer. First, accept that you need a running shoe—your tennis or aerobics shoe is simply not designed for the high-impact and stable rear foot control that you need. Then find out what kind of running shoe is best for you. Read *Runner's World* or *Running Times* magazines for shoe reviews, and visit specialty shops that specialize in running. (There's more on selecting the right running shoes later in the chapter.)

• **Don't run with headphones.** For music lovers, combining the experience of running to Mozart's "Eine kleine Nachtmusik" or U2's "Mysterious Ways" heightens the enjoyment, but for safety reasons, pounding the pavement with your favorite tunes blaring in your ear is not a good idea. Although listening to headphones is fine for treadmill running at home or in the health club, you won't hear approaching traffic, cyclists, dogs, and other hazards on the road.

• **Do wear comfortable running clothes.** If you want to be pegged as a beginner, just show up to your first 5K or group run in black dress socks or perhaps a full sweatsuit in 90-degree weather. Wear something breathable. The human body has a built-in air conditioning system called sweating. Let your body do the job it was designed for by wearing light shorts and singlets (sleeveless T-shirts) and light-colored running clothing that doesn't absorb heat. Running socks should be made of materials like polypropelene that will wick away moisture and keep your feet dry. The wetter your feet, the more likely you'll experience friction-related injuries such as blisters and black toes.

- **Don't be afraid to walk.** If you've never run before, the best way to begin is to run for a few short minutes at a time, and then walk, and then run again as your current fitness allows. Everybody starts out this way, so there's no reason to feel ashamed about it. Even experienced runners training for a marathon intersperse walking breaks during long runs to help their legs recover.

- **Do follow the rules of the road.** Like drivers and cyclists, runners have their own rules of the road. Novices often disobey these rules at the expense of their own safety. The best possible scenario is to avoid running near or around traffic. But when the situation forces you to hit the roadways, use some common sense—run against traffic, not with it. The reasons are simple. When you run with traffic, you can't see what's going on behind you. If a car is weaving all over the road behind you, you have no chance to react.

- **Don't run in dark, isolated areas.** Crime is something we don't like to think about when we run, but the reality is that you've got to take your precautions. We've all heard the horror stories, and instead of becoming one of them, it's in your best interest to stick to running routes that don't put you in jeopardy. After the sun goes down, stay away from secluded parks or trails that may prove dangerous, especially if you live in a high-crime area. Not to sound paranoid, but criminals use the cover of dark and seclusion to set their traps, and you don't want to be the mouse. So run in well-lit, populated areas. If you can't avoid a dark stretch or secluded area, at least have your wits about you and try to anticipate any possible "surprises."

If You're Already a Runner

Of all three sports, the run leg of a triathlon is the one most apt to catch off guard the novice who hasn't trained properly. If you're a veteran runner, believe it or not, the same surprise may be in for you unless you do more than just pound the pavement. Here are some tips for the seasoned harrier:

- **Dive in and hit the road.** Those runner's legs may churn like a steam engine during that Sunday morning 10K, but if you don't balance your training, your legs may feel like rubber after a hard swim and bike ride. Although training in the other two sports will likely cut into your running time, the more balanced approach of multisport training may rejuvenate your road-weary legs.

- **Don't fret about mileage.** Many serious runners count the miles they run as though they were balancing their checkbook. Be prepared to face the fact that your weekly mileage will likely decrease as you add swimming and cycling to your time equation. Don't sweat it. Remember, the goal is balanced training.

- **Follow hard runs with easy bike rides or a swim.** If you're a performance-oriented runner doing hard workouts such as intervals and hills (more on this later), you've probably been following those intense sessions with an easy run the next day. After planning your triathlon training, if you decide to keep doing these tough run workouts, make sure you don't follow them up with a hard bike workout. Apply the same hard / easy principle to multisport training and go for a relatively short and easy ride, or better yet, a swim.

Watching Your Step

By far, most injuries that occur to triathletes happen as a result of running. Although there are several reasons for this, the simplest explanation is that running is very stressful on the body. Every time you put in a hard run, you overstress your muscles. On a physiological level, cells are damaged via tears on the membranes. It sounds pretty scientific, but all it really means is that pounding the pavement puts a pretty good wallop on your legs.

Through the years, runners have found that interspersing running with rest has helped improve the odds of avoiding injury, as well as improving performance. As the popularity of multisports grew, cross-training became an additional tool for helping the body to recover, as well as a way of staying fit without necessarily just running all the time. Inevitably, even the most dedicated runner looks to cross-training to spice things up, which also explains why most triathletes come from a running background. Sometimes the issue is forced, as in the all-too-common running injury. Sometimes the motivation is performance; you can gain only so much improvement by putting in more or faster miles.

Most running injuries are a result of not allowing the body enough rest and recovery time. Planning and following a smart and effective training schedule that builds in rest days and easy training days for recovery is crucial to avoiding injury. The problem is that many runners are bundles of nervous energy when it comes to rest. Running can become an addiction, albeit a healthy addiction. Without the soothing effect of the runner's high, many harriers find themselves out of their element when they take an extended period away from running.

Fortunately for us triathletes, training in more than one activity significantly improves our chances of staying healthy. Cross-training distributes the stress of running over the entire muscle network. No one muscle group is likely to be taxed beyond its limits. For example, marathon runners are particularly susceptible to overuse injurys because of the constant stress and strain of using the same leg muscles, mile after mile.

More than likely, the distance you are training for is in the 5K to 10K range. Although you may not be putting in the miles of a marathoner, these hints will help you train safely and effectively:

• **Build a solid foundation (base).** We'll get more into base training in the next chapter, but it's worth mentioning here that base training is a particularly important component of run training. Running requires muscle strength and involves high cardiovascular and respiratory demands, so it's vital that you progress gradually, taking steps along the way to let your body recover.

• **Follow time, not mileage.** It's far easier to track your running progress using time as your measuring stick, not mileage. You don't have to worry about measuring your running routes, or whether you've put in enough miles for your race goal (which is always a topic of considerable debate anyway). All you have to do is set your sports watch on the countdown timer mode for the desired time of your run. If you have an out-and-back course, set your watch to beep at the halfway point. Tracking time is also much less distracting than counting miles and often helps to avoid excessive mileage that can lead to overtraining or injury.

• **Follow the 10 percent rule.** It's more of a general guideline than a rule, but experts contend that you shouldn't increase your weekly mileage by more than 10 percent. For example, if you've run three times this week for 20 minutes each workout for a total of 60 minutes, next week's running time should not exceed more than 66 minutes. The week after that, you can increase your running time to 73 minutes (10 percent of 66 rounded to the nearest digit is seven additional minutes).

The second vital thing to remember about this rule is that you should *back off* by 10 percent every third or fourth week of training, depending on how well you recover and the length of running time we're talking about. That means you should decrease your running time for one week, and then continue increasing your time again by 10 percent, beginning where you left off. This decrease gives your body a bit of a chance to "catch its breath" from the increases in training and the cumulative stress you've put your legs through for three or four weeks.

Table 6.1 Sample Workout Plan Based on the 10 Percent Rule

	Total running (in minutes)	Increase/decrease (rounded)	% Increase/decrease (rounded)
Week 1	60	—	—
Week 2	66	+6	10%
Week 3	73	+7	10%
Week 4	80	+7	10%
Week 5	72	−8	−10%*
Week 6	88	+8	10%**
Week 7	97	+9	10%
Week 8	107	+10	10%
Week 9	96	−11	−10%*
Week 10	118	+11	10%**

*These are "back-off" weeks when you should decrease your total running time by 10 percent.

**In the week following a "back-off" week, increase your time by 10 percent based on the week prior to a "back-off" week.

If any of this confuses you, or you're not good with numbers, don't sweat it. The main thing you need to remember is to always increase your mileage gradually and put in an easier week of running workouts once every month or so.

• **Plan your workouts accordingly.** Try and plan your running workouts for a day that isn't going to be too close to other hard workouts. For example, if you do a hard cycling ride on Wednesday that leaves your legs feeling like spaghetti, Thursday would not be a good day to put in a long run. Allow yourself an easy day, both before and after any hard runs. If you don't, you're risking injury.

• **Go for consistency.** The most frequent mistake new runners make when training is blowing up after the first few minutes. For every run, make your goal consistency so that your body adapts to prolonged hard efforts (like in a race). You don't teach your body and your mind good pacing by having erratic running workouts that, if you charted the pace, would look like the stock market. Try to maintain an even pace throughout your runs.

• **Concentrate on your form.** Form isn't as crucial in running as in swimming or even cycling, yet good form does make a difference in avoiding injury over the long term. Focusing on form teaches your body to hone in on biomechanical improvements and to run more efficiently. Don't dwell on it too much, especially if you're a beginner. Just keep form in mind when doing your next run.

Concentrate on running relaxed, smoothly, and naturally, without any unusually jarring foot strikes. Everybody has a different running style; try and get a sense for yours, while having an eye out for some possible improvements that may reduce unnecessary stress on knees, hips, and even the upper body muscles. Here are a few quick tips that may help you find your form:

1. Try to minimize excessive bouncing motion.
2. Relax your upper body, especially the shoulders.
3. Find the stride length and cadence (number of steps you take to cover a distance) that you feel comfortable with.

• **Make it enjoyable.** Running workouts can be enjoyable. (Okay, stop laughing. I'm being semi-serious here.) Group runs can make training a social experience. The drawback is that you won't get a workout specific to your training goal, but you can always duck out if it's too long or run longer if it's too short.

Overcoming a Mental Running Block

You may be used to running a mile every now and then, just to stay in shape. But when you start considering longer distances, you may find your biggest obstacle isn't your body, but your mind. That's exactly what happened to FD Moore when he tried to go beyond a mile. Working for the U.S. Army as a civilian overseas in 1989, he would run four laps around a quarter-mile track just to keep in shape. But when he sought to expand his endurance horizons, he just couldn't make it happen.

"I had this mental block that kept me from running any farther," says the 34-year-old triathlete from Manassas, Virginia. "I just couldn't envision running any more than four laps, and it affected my body. I felt fatigued and tired every time I attempted more than four laps, even though I was in good enough shape to run more."

One day he decided to train on a different track on another army base. The change of environment is what he needed to get over that hump. He ran 6 laps, then 8, then 12, finally finishing the workout with three miles, more than he had ever run in his life. "Once I did that," says FD, "I realized my potential." That realization led FD to add mountain biking, and then road riding, to his training. He completed his first duathlon in 1992 and completed a sprint distance triathlon two years later.

FD has three running tips if you find yourself struggling with the thought of running longer distances: "Try changing your typical running route. Also run with running clubs. When you're around other people, you lose track of the miles, and before you know it, you've run farther than you ever have. And set a road race goal, like a 5K, you want to achieve later in the season. When you train, set realistic mini-goals as stepping stones to help you finish your 5K."

Finding the Shoe That Fits

In *The Complete Book of Running*, New York City Marathon organizer Fred Lebow quotes a sports medicine podiatrist as saying, "Running shoes are like lovers. There is no one type for everyone, but when you find yours, you're set for life. Stick with it."

Finding the right shoe for the unique size, shape, and structure of your feet is one of the primary steps you need to take to cut down on foot problems. However, finding the perfect fit can be a daunting task. Invariably, questions regarding running gait arise. Should you get a shoe that will control your overpronation (when your foot rolls inward too much)? What if you need something that controls oversupination (when your foot rolls outward too much)?

"Most runners are obsessed with whether they supinate or pronate," says Dr. George Tsatsos, a sports medicine physician with a specialty in podiatry and a consultant to the American Running and Fitness Association. "A little bit of supination or pronation is normal, but many runners walk into a shoe store and buy shoes based on an incorrect self-diagnosis. This can result in buying the wrong shoe for your feet and the subsequent foot problems that come with that."

Here are some shopping recommendations that Dr. Tsatsos says will help you find the best-fitting pair of running shoes for your feet:

Running in the correct shoe can be the difference between running your best, or sustaining an injury.

- Look for uneven pressure points when you're trying on your new shoes, especially in the toe area.
- Make sure the heel support is relatively stiff and firm.
- After lacing the shoe correctly, check for any excess movement or looseness.

"When you go to shop for a new shoe, make sure that you go during the middle or end of the day," adds Dr. Lawrence Burns, a sports medicine podiatrist. "You should do this because your feet swell somewhat after prolonged pressure from standing and walking. This will ensure that you get the right size shoe. If the salesperson measures your foot, make sure you are standing."

Running in the Heat

Although heat can be a problem in any of the three sports, it is the biggest obstacle in running. Water is a natural coolant during a swim, and the wind in cycling does provide some cooling effect (although most of the tips here also apply to cycling in the heat).

Running in searing heat can be unpleasant. The sun beats down upon your sweaty brow, the humidity factor makes it feel as though you're breathing pea soup, and your running shoes stick to sizzling asphalt. Worst of all, running in high temperatures can be dangerous. The key to avoiding these hot-weather dangers is careful planning and preparation. Abiding by these few common-sense running tips will keep you from being a summertime triathlon training casualty:

- **Become acclimatized.** If you haven't already done it, the first thing you need to do when the mercury begins to soar is adjust your training pace. Too many triathletes expect to maintain the same intensity in their workouts without allowing their bodies an opportunity to adapt to the heat. Your body will eventually adjust to the heat with regular exercise in hot conditions. Some of these heat adaptations include improved blood flow to the skin, higher heart rate, decreased perspiration, and less salt loss in sweat. This period of adjustment, or acclimatization, usually takes about 10 days of workouts strung together in similar conditions.

- **Avoid the ozone zone.** Perhaps the best way of beating the heat is avoiding it altogether. That means planning your runs for a time of day when temperatures are at their lowest, such as early in the morning or later in the evening. Another variable is the air quality, which tends to worsen as the temperature rises. If you live in a congested area and are frequently forced to run in close proximity to traffic during midday hours, you could be hurting your health, not helping it.

"Since your breathing increases dramatically when you exercise, you will breathe more harmful chemicals when exercising in a polluted environment," states a pamphlet on safe running published by the American Running & Fitness Association (ARFA). In one cited study, athletes who ran in a polluted area had three times the concentration of harmful chemicals in their bloodstream than the average population in this area, equivalent to smoking 10 to 20 cigarettes a day. ARFA recommends running in the morning, when the air quality is best, or after rush hour. Ozone levels begin to increase soon after dawn and peak at around noon and early afternoon, so avoid running at midday.

• **Wear light clothing.** Choose your clothing carefully. Wear light colors and use a sleeveless running singlet or lightweight T-shirt. Men should never run without a top (unless in a shaded area) to avoid sunburn. Use running shorts designed with slits on the side for ventilation and made from materials, such as Coolmax®, that wick away moisture.

• **Protect yourself from the sun.** One of the biggest dangers in being outside is the effects of sun on the skin. UV light causes irreversible skin damage and skin aging, not to mention the increased likelihood of skin cancer. In addition to the previous clothing tips, here is some more advice from the Skin Cancer Foundation:

1. Apply a sunscreen with sun protection factor (SPF) of 15 or greater before every run, even on overcast days.
2. Wear sunglasses that shield your eyes from harmful UV rays.
3. Use a visor or hat with a mesh top to allow for heat dissipation from the top of your head.
4. Beware of reflective surfaces such as sand, concrete, and water, which can reflect more than half the sun's rays onto your skin.

• **Drink plenty of fluids.** The biggest key to avoiding dehydration and heat illness is to stay properly hydrated. Make sure to drink eight ounces of water or a sports drink every 15 minutes while you

Your first priority after a hot run or race should be to replenish fluids.

run. Either plan your route so that you have a water fountain or convenience store stop along the way (make sure you bring money), or bring some fluid along with you. I wouldn't recommend carrying a water bottle in your hand as you run (it throws off your stride, and it's damn annoying). But plenty of products, such as water belts, water bottle holders, and the Camelbak®, make it easier to bring along some fluids.

Hydrate before and after each run. If you drive to a running trail, drink fluids on the way there and bring along a small cooler so that your favorite carbohydrate beverage is nice and cold after your run. Because dehydration is potentially fatal and typically misunderstood among novice runners, you'll find further information on fluids and avoiding heat illnesses in chapter 8.

Your Running Repertoire

If you think running is just a matter of keeping your legs moving, you need to expand your training repertoire to include a variety of different kinds of runs. You've got your fartlek, track intervals, hill

Racing Tip

Fortunately, any well-organized race will have aid stations on the run course where you can fill up with water or sport drinks. You should drink at every aid station (especially if it's hot), but competitors differ on whether to continue to run, or walk while drinking. Your choice should depend on your race goal. If time is not a big concern, a brief period of walking while you sip on Gatorade® will help your legs recover. If you do decide to hydrate on the fly, grab the paper cup and squeeze the top of the cup to keep fluids from spilling. Squeeze the brim enough to form a V shape; this will form a funnel for easy drinking while running.

workouts, and good ole LSD (no, not the drug; it stands for long slow distance, wise guy). You've got trail runs, flat runs, hilly runs, short runs, long runs, tempo runs—all kinds of ways to put one foot in front of the other.

It's good to have an awareness of your choices, but not every training technique mentioned here is a good option for the beginner or newcomer. The following sections describe a few types of workouts that might be helpful in making sure you've got something left in your legs at the end of a race.

Long Slow Distance

Once a week, do long, steady runs at an easy, comfortable intensity or at a pace that could be considered "comfortably hard." (Isn't that an oxymoron?) These runs should be conducted at a pace that can be maintained for an hour or two without undue respiratory stress—in other words, without sounding as though you're having a heart attack. Practically speaking, this run is the typical long, conversational run that groups of runners often get together for on a weekend morning. (After which, they partake in a ritualistic pancakes, sausage, and scrambled eggs platter at Denny's.)

Some experts contend that you should be working at what you perceive to be 60 to 70 percent of your perceived maximum effort, but some research has indicated that a range of 50 to 60 percent is just as beneficial. If you're like me and have no idea what that means, your best bet is to listen for your breath—if you can hear yourself laboring, you're going too fast. This low-intensity approach, coupled with a long continuous effort, is ideal for developing the cardiovascular system, improving the blood flow in active muscles, and building overall fitness and strength.

Tempo Running

Tempo running is when you run alongside a Ford Tempo for as long as you can (just kidding). Seriously, tempo running is running at a fairly fast pace that you can maintain for 20 to 30 minutes and that is 15 to 20 seconds slower than your fastest 10K pace. Sometimes these runs are referred to in running jargon as "lactic acid threshold" workouts.

The purpose of tempo runs is to take your body to the edge of what's called your lactate threshold, which is the point beyond which lactic acid begins accumulating in the blood at a more rapid rate than normal. You may have experienced going beyond your lactic threshold when climbing a hill or getting on a Stairmaster® and feeling a burn in your thighs. Tempo runs are designed to push your threshold further and further away so that eventually your body is able to tolerate a faster pace without lactic acid buildup. If physiological jargon scares you, think of these runs as performance boosters that are helping to raise the pace threshold your body can maintain for a distance.

Tempo runs should be steadily paced runs, slightly slower than the speed with which you might run a road race of the distance you're training for. Tempo runs stress your body to a certain point—not less, not more. Keep in mind that hills, uneven footing, and strong winds can affect intensity, so try to run tempo runs on a flat, even course.

Fartlek

Fartlek is a Swedish word meaning speedplay. These medium-distance runs include random and relatively short bursts of speed in the middle miles, thrown in to help break up the monotony. In addition to the mental break fartlek runs provide, they are also a good way of playing with your body, seeing how fast you can make it to the next light pole and how quick you recover from the effort. A fartlek run can be almost anything, from running hard every other block to racing your training partner to the next water fountain. Keep in mind, however, that these bursts of speed should be kept under control and should not dominate your workout as they do in interval training (see the later section on this topic). The speedplay should be sparse, relatively short, and never executed as an all-out sprint.

Hilly Workouts

Running hills is a great way to intensify your workouts. Running uphill is an excellent workout for your hamstring muscles and running downhill increases coordination skills and strengthens vital quadricep muscles. Like any type of higher intensity training tool, however, running hills should be approached cautiously. Without a proper running base, a safe course, and the right technique, hill running may cause injuries such as shin splints, calf tears, and knee soreness. If you are ready for hilly workouts, pay special attention to your uphilll and downhill running technique. Proper form will help you finish these workouts safely.

Here are some quick technique tips for running uphill:

- Shorten your stride.
- Lean into the hill.
- Keep your arms low for better balance.
- Pump your arms (but don't exaggerate the motion).

When running downhill, follow these guidelines:

- Lengthen your stride.
- Don't put the brakes on by leaning backwards or shortening your stride (unless you have to).
- Keep your arms higher for better balance.

Interval Training
(Not Recommended for the Beginner)

Interval workouts are a form of speedwork, a running term used to describe high-intensity workouts designed to improve performance. Speedwork is not recommended for the running beginner; the stress and strain these types of workouts put on your legs is tremendous, and these workouts require a greater foundation of training than is typical of the novice.

As was mentioned in the swimming chapter, intervals are repeated, short bursts of speed over a measured distance. Running intervals are usually done on a track, with recovery periods of either walking or relaxed jogging in between each interval. The purpose of interval running is to increase your maximum oxygen uptake, and the faster running teaches your body to be more biomechanically efficient.

Running With Troy

Troy Jacobson has been a competitive triathlete for 11 years, a coach for 7 years, and a professional for 2 years. He has participated in over 150 triathlons, garnering over 40 victories. Although he continues to compete professionally, he also coaches triathletes in Baltimore and through an Internet service (see the appendix for his address). "I've got a good mix of beginners, middle-of-the-packers, and professionals that I coach," says the 30-year-old triathlete pro and coach. "I really enjoy working with triathletes training for their first race. My goal is to get them on the right track from the start."

Troy loves to race long distances. He has won the USA Triathlon Long Course (half-Ironman) Championship two years in a row (1997

Professional triathlete and coach Troy Jacobson taking top honors at the hotly contested Gulf Coast Triathlon.

to 1998). He's raced the Hawaiian Ironman Triathlon Championship five times and completed the race once in under nine hours (an impressive milestone for professionals). Although triathlon is his sport, Troy is also an talented distance runner in his own right. He holds a PR (personal record) time of 2:31 in the marathon. With Troy's extensive background in racing and coaching, I've asked him to answer some of the most common questions novice triathletes ask about run training.

Expert Q & A

There's always a ton of questions on beginning triathletes' minds when they come to me for running advice. I'm glad to be able to answer here some of the most common questions, which I've put together from my first-hand experience. The questions come from beginners ranging from little athletic background to those who have more running experience.

Q: What can I do to improve how I feel coming off the bike?

A: First, make sure you put in a solid base of running. If you're not a huge fan of running, you may try to avoid it as much as possible, but that kind of approach will do you in at the end of a triathlon. Second, brick workouts that combine biking and running are very helpful. (You'll find more on bricks in the next chapter.) Third, during the race, take little steps in the first half-mile to minimize the discomfort and stretch out the leg muscles. Gradually increase your stride until you're running normally.

Q: How many miles should I be putting in a week?

A: Most of my beginners are training for a sprint or Olympic distance race and average about 15 to 20 miles a week. However, I don't recommend you go by miles as much as time. Time is a more controllable variable and much easier to measure.

Q: I've heard so much about intervals. Should I be doing these kinds of workouts?

A: Interval workouts are for more advanced and performance-oriented runners. If you're just beginning and simply want to finish a race, your running should be done at an aerobic pace, which means a comfortable intensity. The most common mistake I see triathletes make is running too hard. This "no pain, no gain" mentality is just ridiculous. Many beginners I coach think that they need to do intense runs, like intervals, to gain any benefit. That's simply not true.

Sometimes impatience and competitiveness can get in the way too. I have a few triathletes who not only want to get fit, they want to get faster in a hurry, which normally takes years of advanced training. If your competitive juices are flowing, it's important to realize that you need to take it one step at a time in order to avoid injury and progress safely.

Q: What's a comfortable pace?

A: It's different for everyone and I work one-on-one with my athletes to access their typical running pace and where their comfort zone is. But generally, if you take a perceived exertion level of 1 to 10, with 10 being your maximum effort for a three-mile run, I find aerobic running usually falls somewhere around 6.

Q: I'm always getting injured. What can I do to avoid injury?

A: I get many beginners who are either coming back from an injury or have chronic leg problems from running. Sports medicine is not my area of expertise, so I refer athletes having injury problems to a sports clinic in my area that offers a very sophisticated computerized running gait analysis. Using digital cameras, they take a close look at how you run and how your stride may be contributing to injury, and then provide recommendations. If you have a similar facility in your area, I strongly advise that you use it. If not, at least go to a running specialty store to find the right shoe and try to do most of your workouts on trails and other soft surfaces.

Chapter 7

Training for All Three

> "When all is said and done, the only pressure you have is what you generate for yourself."
>
> —Paula Newby-Fraser, eight-time Ironman champion

How's your balancing act? At work, are you good at juggling two or more projects or tasks at one time, or do you find yourself leaning toward one and neglecting the others? Do you have a good balance between your family and career, or does your home life suffer because you don't spend enough time with your spouse and kids?

What do all these questions have to do with triathlon training? Well, in many ways, your success in putting together three distinct exercise activities into one solid training program will depend on how skilled you are at balancing. Sure, we'll go over some practical tips in this chapter, such as how to create a functional training schedule and how to bike off the swim and run off the bike. But ultimately, your success will hinge on your mental approach to the sport and how well you understand the significance of balancing.

Take a quick mental inventory of your success in balancing other aspects of your life. Do you have a tendency to take things a bit too far? If that's the case, maybe your learning experience with triathlon will improve much more than just your fitness.

Triathlon Training Do's and Don'ts

Good training is not just about listening to your body, although that's certainly important. It's also about learning to listen to your family, and your boss, and the voice in your head that keeps telling you to take it easy on yourself. The following list of do's and don'ts will help you get the most out of your triathlon training:

• **Do add variety.** Try not to do the same thing all the time—reach for new goals and more challenges. Change your running course, or better yet, take the family to a weekend getaway, preferably somewhere where you can still get in some good training. That way you can combine family values with your triathlon goal.

• **Don't sacrifice your family or career.** Stick to your priorities. Triathlon training should be a solid addition to a well-balanced lifestyle, not an obsession that hinders your family life or puts your career in danger. Besides, your chances of succeeding in triathlon—whatever that means to you—will be greatly increased if you have the support of your family and coworkers.

• **Do be realistic about your available time.** There's nothing worse than constantly checking your watch during a workout. Part of the reason for working out is for stress relief, so why not schedule your workouts during a time of day when you won't feel hurried? Overestimating how much time you can afford to spend on training can lead to feeling rushed and frustrated and can also contribute to a faster pace when you know you should be going slower.

• **Don't be inflexible.** Don't be so rigid in executing your training that you endanger your health or neglect your other priorities. If your training schedule seems to be too hard on your body, rethink your approach and build in some more recovery days, or cut the distance or intensity.

Workouts in Hell #73: training partners.

• **Do follow the hard/easy rule.** Working at a high intensity all the time will only increase your chances of injury. Always make sure you give your body a chance to recover, especially from hard or long runs, with easy workouts the day following a hard one.

Training in Phases

In chapter 2, we took a brief look at the various training phases recommended for the beginner. As you recall, training in phases (or cycles) allows you to focus on one component of your training for an extended period of time. This type of training ensures that you progress safely and gradually. After all, there's no such thing as overnight fitness.

The following is a more complete description of each of these phases, followed by some sample workout schedules that incorporate all three disciplines. These sample training schedules differ according to each phase. If you haven't already divided your training schedule into these phases, now would be a good time to do so. Or if you'd like, photocopy the blank training grids at the end of this book and use them to plan your training in phases.

These schedules should be viewed as templates or general guidelines to setting up your unique training plan. Devising a training schedule can be a frustrating experience if you don't have any guidelines. Add to this the anxiety of recurring questions of diet, equipment choices, and the optimum race schedule, and things can get pretty complicated.

You'll notice only the sprint and Olympic distances are covered here. That's because the vast majority of beginners and novice triathletes do (and should) start at the sprint distance and progress to the Olympic distance. Some athletes, especially endurance veterans who already have a high degree of proficiency in one or more of the three disciplines, choose to start with an Olympic distance race. (Although there are several awe-inspiring cases of newcomers taking on the half-Ironman or Ironman distances, it's not generally recommended.)

These training templates are loosely based on the key workout method pioneered by eight-time Ironman triathlon champion Paula Newby-Fraser. If you're interested in not just finishing a triathlon, but doing well, this approach includes one workout in each sport that is specifically designed to achieve the objective of each phase. Of course, feel free to substitute similar workouts that result in the same training effect. You'll also find some general recommendations on alternative workouts and ideas to mix things up a bit.

Some workouts are optional. Gauge how you feel on those days. If there are signs of overtraining, such as elevated heart rate, moodiness, and joint fatigue, back off and take a recovery day. It's a good idea anyway to take off at least one day a week, to provide you with a mental and physical lift. In the following sample workout schedules, you'll notice that Monday is earmarked for recovery. That's because, in most cases, the longest or hardest workouts will fall on weekends. Thus Mondays allow you to recover from these workouts and start fresh for another week of triathlon training.

Many of the swimming workouts focus on drills. That's because, as we discussed in chapter 4, a common mistake too many triathletes make is putting in too many laps without executing proper technique. Unlike running and biking, swimming depends heavily on technique. Remember, drills can help you unlearn bad habits and swim more efficiently.

The Initiation Phase (Beginners Only)

If you're starting from square one with very little or no endurance training experience in either swimming, cycling, or running, you'll have to apportion a time period in your training calendar for getting your feet wet, literally and figuratively, in multisports. (If you have a good or above-average endurance training background in all three sports, congratulations! You get to skip to the next phase.)

This phase may try your patience because you'll be learning at least one activity that you've never attempted before. In order for you to learn safely, workouts will usually be brief (though your muscles may feel as if they've gone a lot longer). It is a time for your body to adapt gradually to new activity and to overcome the inevitable discomforts that go with triathlon training. It may take you weeks to swim one lap without hugging the wall, ride three miles without feeling as though your butt has been caned, and run around the block without feeling as though your lungs are going to explode. But be patient. Your body does have a remarkable ability to adapt. The crucial thing to remember in this phase, as with all the phases, is that good things will come to triathletes who are kind to their bodies.

Here are some things you should know about the initiation phase:

- This phase can last one to three months, depending on how quickly you learn and how well your body adapts.

- If you're new to swimming, this phase will consist of a beginner's swimming class and at least two to three workouts per week on your own to perform drills learned in that class.
- If you're new to cycling or running, this phase will consist of short, easy workouts with plenty of recovery time in between.
- The patience of a saint is required, especially if you're just learning to swim.

The following sample workout schedules are examples of initiation training for beginners to swimming, cycling, and running.

Initiation to Swimming
Sample Workout Schedule

SWIMMING	**Mon**	Off
	Tue	**Key workout:** beginner's swim class
	Wed	Practice drills learned in this week's class for 20 min
	Thu	Off
	Fri	Practice drills learned in this week's class for 30 min
	Sat	Off
	Sun	Practice drills learned in this week's class for 30 min

Initiation to Cycling
Sample Workout Schedule

CYCLING	**Mon**	Off
	Tue	15 to 20 min of easy spinning
	Wed	Off
	Thu	15 to 20 min of easy spinning
	Fri	Off
	Sat	**Key workout:** 30 min of easy spinning with a rest stop halfway (if necessary)
	Sun	Off

Initiation to Running
Sample Workout Schedule

RUNNING		
	Mon	Off
	Tue	2 min of easy running and 1 min of walking; do this 5 times
	Wed	Off
	Thu	2 min of easy running and 1 min of walking; do this 5 times
	Fri	Off
	Sat	Off
	Sun	**Key workout:** 5 min of easy running and 2 min of walking; do this 2 times

The following are some things to keep in mind during this phase.

- If you are new to more than one sport, you will need to combine two or three schedules into one that works for you.
- For the sports in which the initiation phase is not required, refer to the Base Training Workout Schedule for guidance.
- If you're a beginning swimmer, it's especially important to work on the weekly lessons and drills independently of your swimming class.

The Base Phase

Look at this base period of training as the foundation of a building. When construction contractors build a home or office building, a large portion of the overall project time is spent ensuring that the foundation is solid and stable. Once that's done, the rest of the building goes up relatively quickly.

The same can be said of base training for endurance sports. This is the phase that, if executed properly, may take the longest. But the long-term rewards are injury prevention, greater performance, and healthy balance. It's worth noting that, if your goal is just to finish a race, your workouts may consist almost entirely of base training. That's just fine. As long as you have a solid foundation, just finishing is a realistic goal.

Here are some things to keep in mind about base training.

- It can last from three to six months, depending on your current conditioning, skills, and the distance for which you are training.
- This phase consists mainly of long workouts done at a slow pace.
- Your focus should be on gradual increases of workout length of no more than 10 percent per week, a rule that is especially crucial for running (discussed in chapter 6) and helps avoid common overtraining injuries.

Refer to the sample base training workout schedule for the sprint distance on next page.

The following are some training tips for this phase:

- Your running and cycling workouts should be conducted at a conversational, easy pace; if your breathing is labored, you're going too fast.
- If your current workout in a given sport isn't within the time ranges given in the Sample Workout Schedule, work on gradually increasing your training using the 10 percent rule explained in chapter 6.
- Remember, spinning means keeping your RPMs at 85 to 95. If you don't have a bike computer or one with a cadence feature, try to always ride in a gear that is not too hard.
- Run on a soft surface, such as wilderness trails, to avoid knee problems. Watch for dips in trails and chipmunk holes so you don't twist an ankle.

The Speed and Technique Phase

Remember the Six Million Dollar Man? Television astronaut Steve Austin splatters himself all over a runway and gets a government grant for six big bills to make him "better, stronger." Well, that's sort of the idea with speed and technique training—minus the splattering, six million bucks, and the bionics.

You may not be at all concerned at how fast you stroke, pedal, or put one foot in front of the other. Good for you. If your next triathlon will be your first, the best thing you can do for yourself is dismiss any expectations you have of finishing at a certain time. Do it simply to finish. Period.

Base Training Sample Workout Schedule (Sprint Distance)

SWIMMING	Mon	Off
	Tue	30 min of drill practice
	Wed	Off
	Thu	**Key workout:** 10 × 50 yd intervals with 30 s rest
	Fri	30 min of drill practice
	Sat	Off
	Sun	400 m easy swimming with some drill sets (optional)
CYCLING	Mon	Off
	Tue	30 min of easy spinning
	Wed	30-45 min of easy spinning
	Thu	Off
	Fri	30 min of easy spinning (optional)
	Sat	**Key workout:** work up to a 60 min ride
	Sun	Off
RUNNING	Mon	Off
	Tue	Off
	Wed	15 min of easy running
	Thu	20 min tempo run
	Fri	15 min easy running
	Sat	Off
	Sun	**Key workout:** walk up to a 30 to 45 min easy run with 2-min walking breaks (if necessary)

But if you have a few multisport events under your belt already, speed and technique workouts can help you hone your skills for safer, more efficient training. If that doesn't motivate you, how about the prospect of finishing a triathlon without feeling like you've just been run over by a steamroller?

That said, don't make too much out of these workouts. Speedwork, such as interval training on a running track, can wreak havoc on your body. It's a frequently confusing and misunderstood topic, particularly for the novice, and can often lead to injury. In summary, if the reason behind your race goal is to improve upon a previous time and achieve greater performance, then this phase is key. If your goal is to complete your first triathlon and just to finish, skip it.

Here are some things to keep in mind about speed and technique training.

- It can last from three weeks to several months, depending on your current conditioning and performance goals.
- This phase consists of a select few (one per week in each sport, max) high-intensity workouts designed to increase cardiovascular and mechanical efficiency.
- Speedwork can easily lead to injury if base training has not been properly executed. Don't progress to speedwork until you have been finishing long, slow workouts for a period of at least three months.

See next page for a sample workout schedule for speed and technique training.

The following are some workout tips for speed and technique training.

- Always ease into a workout. Make sure to do a proper warm-up before long or hard sessions, such as the key workouts.
- If you are an experienced runner, you can replace the fartlek session with a track interval workout: run a slow one-mile warm-up; run six quarter-mile intervals at your 5K pace with 30 seconds recovery after each; run a slow one-mile cool-down.

The Race Simulation Phase

Among the biggest concerns for the beginner looking to complete his or her first triathlon is the mystery that awaits all first-time triathletes on that fateful day. Questions inevitably arise, many of them associated with transitioning from one sport to the other and the transition's effects on the body:

Speed and Technique Phase
Sample Workout Schedule

SWIMMING	**Mon**	Off
	Tue	**Key workout:** 10 × 50 yd intervals with 15 s rest
	Wed	30 min of drill practice
	Thu	Off
	Fri	400 m easy swimming and 15 min of drill sets
	Sat	Off
	Sun	400 m easy swimming with some drill sets (optional)
CYCLING	**Mon**	Off
	Tue	30 min of easy spinning
	Wed	Off
	Thu	**Key workout:** 45 min ride on a challenging, hilly course
	Fri	30 min of easy spinning (optional)
	Sat	60 min easy ride
	Sun	Off
RUNNING	**Mon**	Off
	Tue	Off
	Wed	15 min of easy running
	Thu	Off
	Fri	20 min tempo run
	Sat	Off
	Sun	**Key workout:** 30 min fartlek run

- How am I going to feel coming out of the water?
- How do I handle the transitions?
- What if my muscles cramp going from the bike to the run?

That last question is a legitimate concern. Most triathletes will agree that the toughest transition is from bike to run, especially if

USA Triathlon rules require you to buckle your helmet before you get on the bike, or face disqualification.

your cycling leg has been especially intense or hilly. Even if you've taken it easy on the bike, you may find yourself starting the run feeling like the gears are turning, but you're going nowhere. Prepare yourself for this unsettling sensation during the bike-to-run transition, but also realize that all you need is a little practice, some encouragement, and confidence.

Race training is designed not necessarily to improve your performance in a race (although that might be an incidental effect) but to give you the confidence and encouragement you need. Workouts known as "bricks" combine two sports in a single session and are instrumental to any racing success. By completing workouts that are specifically designed to simulate what you will be experiencing during a race, the shroud of mystery surrounding your upcoming first triathlon will soon begin to evaporate. If you're looking to improve upon previous performances or lengthen your distances, race simulation training will help you do that as well.

Here are some things to keep in mind about this training phase.

- It can last one to two months, depending on your current conditioning and race goals.
- This phase consists of workouts designed to simulate transitions and race conditions, such as bricks that combine two activities in succession and certain key workouts.
- Race simulation can help you hone your transitioning skills.

See the following page for examples of race simulation workouts for the sprint distance.

Here are some additional things to keep in mind for race simulation workouts:

- Make sure to notify the lifeguard on duty before your open water swim.
- Do your bike time trial on a course with little or no traffic or stoplights.

Brick workouts will help you hone your transition skills and improve your race time.

Race Simulation Phase Sample Workout Schedule (Sprint Distance)

SWIMMING	**Mon**	Off
	Tue	**Brick:** 500 m swim (open water strongly recommended) with transition to bike and 30 min of easy spinning
	Wed	40 min of drill practice
	Thu	Off
	Fri	400 m easy swimming and drill sets
	Sat	30 min of drill practice
	Sun	Off
CYCLING	**Mon**	Off
	Tue	**Brick:** 500 m swim (open water strongly recommended) with transition to bike and 30 min of easy spinning
	Wed	Off
	Thu	**Key workout:** 30 min time trial ride at or near race pace
	Fri	45 min of easy spinning
	Sat	Off
	Sun	**Brick:** 45 min easy ride followed by an immediate transition to a 20 min tempo run (or) **Advanced brick:** 30 min hilly or fast-paced ride followed by an immediate transition to a 20 min tempo run
RUNNING	**Mon**	Off
	Tue	Off
	Wed	15 min of easy running
	Thu	Off
	Fri	20 min tempo run
	Sat	Off
	Sun	**Brick:** 45 min easy ride followed by an immediate transition to a 20 min tempo run (or) **Advanced brick:** 30 min hilly or fast-paced ride followed by an immediate transition to a 20 min tempo run

- If you'd like, substitute the bike time trial with a fast and competitive group ride.

- For your brick workouts, prepare a mock transition area, making the transition as you would in a race.

- The Advanced Brick workout is a secondary option. If you complete the Brick workouts with little or no difficulty on several occasions, try this somewhat harder (though shorter) workout. This session should accurately reproduce how you might feel coming off the bike in the race—just make sure you take the run nice and easy.

- Drink plenty of fluids—doing so will minimize the chances of cramping during the bike-to-run transition.

Big on Bricks

When Joe Albert started competing in triathlons in 1996, the toughest part of each race for him was the first mile of the run. Having just made inroads into endurance exercise in the previous year, he found he had a natural talent for running. Unfortunately, that talent went down the tubes every time he came off the bike. "It was just excruciating," says the 32-year-old resident of Plainfield, Illinois. "It was just mentally and physically tough for me, and I just couldn't run like I knew I could when I came off the bike."

With average mile times (splits) hovering around seven and a half minutes for his triathlon run leg (a pace he considered slow), Joe set out to bring those times down. He learned from triathlon training books about bricks and began practicing one bike-to-run workout once a week. The results? During his second year of triathlon competition, his average triathlon run splits have come down to under six minute-miles, a dramatic 90 second-per-mile improvement.

"I think most people have a problem getting into a good running stride after cycling," says Joe. "I figure if I can get into that stride right away, as opposed to a mile or two later, I can have a competitive advantage. Bricks definitely help me do that."

The Tapering Phase

Tapering is a term that's used to describe a period of decreased activity in the days or weeks prior to an athletic event. The purpose of tapering is to give your body ample time to recover from the previous months of training so that you feel mentally fresh and your muscles are primed for racing.

Although there is much debate about the "perfect" tapering schedule, it really all depends on how fast your body recovers from training, how long you've been training, and what you are training for. And although there may be some disagreement about how to taper, experts do concur that you need to taper in order to perform your best. After all, the last thing you want to be is standing on the beach waiting for the start, with your legs feeling sore.

If you taper correctly, your body should feel refreshed and ready to go when you hit the beach.

Here are some things you should know about tapering:

- For a sprint or Olympic distance race, tapering usually encompasses the week prior to your event goal.
- Tapering consists of shorter, easy workouts and may also incorporate more rest days.
- Tapering has benefits for both the first-timer and the veteran triathlete.

The following are a few tips to help you feel fresh on race day.

- Increase your consumption of carbohydrates during tapering.
- Make sure to get plenty of sleep and relaxation.
- If you get a massage, make sure to schedule it at least a week to five days before the race to avoid possible soreness from deep tissue work.

It doesn't make much difference exactly what your workouts consist of in the week prior to an event. What does make a difference is the amount of exercise you perform (or more to the point, the amount you *don't* perform) and the low intensity of the workouts. That's why the tapering charts on the following page provide a recommended total workout time (the total amount of time spent on any one or combination of three sports in one day).

There are two charts, one for tapering over a full week (table 7.1) and another for tapering three days prior to an event (table 7.2). If you have a tendency to take a long time to recover from a workout, it's best if you go with a one-week taper. If you tend to recover pretty quickly, then you'll probably do just fine tapering three days before the event.

Going for Olympic Glory

Although the sprint distance is perfect for the beginner or time-limited triathlete, the Olympic distance is ideal for those who wish to push the endurance envelope beyond the two-hour boundary. It is also a good stepping stone after completing a few sprint distance races.

Following are a set of sample workout schedules for the Olympic distance. Once again, they are divided into phases, so most of the same principles and tips from the sprint distance workouts apply. They are similar to the sprint distance sample workouts (although obviously the distances are longer) with one notable exception: the

Table 7.1 One-Week Taper

Day 1	40 min
Day 2	Complete rest
Day 3	40 min
Day 4	20 min
Day 5	20 min
Day 6	Complete rest
Day 7	RACE DAY

Table 7.2 Half-Week Taper

Day 1	40 min
Day 2	20 min
Day 3	Complete rest
Day 4	RACE DAY

Tapering Phase includes only one option, a full week's taper (see table 7.3 on page 130). Because the training distances are greater for an Olympic distance race, a full week's taper (as opposed to a half-week taper) will give your body the time it needs to recover and feel fresh on the starting line.

Base Training Sample Workout Schedule (Olympic Distance)

SWIMMING	Mon	Off
	Tue	30 min of drill practice
	Wed	Off
	Thu	**Key workout:** 10 $\times$ 100 yd intervals with 15 s rest
	Fri	30 min of drill practice
	Sat	Off
	Sun	800 m easy swimming with some drill sets (optional)
CYCLING	Mon	Off
	Tue	45 min of easy spinning
	Wed	60 min of easy spinning
	Thu	Off
	Fri	45 min of easy spinning (optional)
	Sat	**Key workout:** work up to 90 min to 120 min easy ride
	Sun	Off
RUNNING	Mon	Off
	Tue	Off
	Wed	25 min of easy running
	Thu	30 min tempo run (optional)
	Fri	25 min easy run
	Sat	Off
	Sun	**Key workout:** work up to 60 min to 90 min slow run with a 5 min walking break (if necessary)

Speed and Technique Phase Sample Workout Schedule (Olympic Distance)

SWIMMING	Mon	Off
	Tue	**Key workout:** 10 × 100 m intervals with 10 s rest
	Wed	30 min of drill practice
	Thu	Off
	Fri	800 m easy swimming and 15 min drill sets
	Sat	Off
	Sun	800 m easy swimming with some drill sets (optional)
CYCLING	Mon	Off
	Tue	45 min of easy spinning
	Wed	Off
	Thu	**Key workout:** 60 min ride on a challenging, hilly course
	Fri	45 min of easy spinning (optional)
	Sat	90 min easy ride
	Sun	Off
RUNNING	Mon	Off
	Tue	Off
	Wed	25 min of easy running
	Thu	Off
	Fri	30 min tempo run
	Sat	Off
	Sun	**Key workout:** 40 min fartlek run

Race Simulation Phase Sample
Workout Schedule (Olympic Distance)

SWIMMING	Mon	Off
	Tue	**Brick:** 1000 m swim (open water strongly recommended) with transition to bike and 45 min of easy spinning
	Wed	40 min of drill practice
	Thu	Off
	Fri	800 m easy swimming and drill sets
	Sat	30 min of drill practice
	Sun	Off
CYCLING	Mon	Off
	Tue	**Brick:** 1000 m swim (open water strongly recommended) with transition to bike and 45 min of easy spinning
	Wed	Off
	Thu	**Key workout:** 45 min–60 min time trial ride at or near race pace
	Fri	60 min of easy spinning (optional)
	Sat	Off
	Sun	**Brick:** 45 min hilly or fast-paced ride followed by an immediate transition to a 30 min easy run
RUNNING	Mon	Off
	Tue	Off
	Wed	25 min of easy running
	Thu	Off
	Fri	30 min tempo run
	Sat	Off
	Sun	**Brick:** 45 min hilly or fast-paced ride followed by an immediate transition to a 30 min easy run

Table 7.3 One-Week Taper (Olympic Distance)

Day 1	60 min
Day 2	Complete rest
Day 3	40 min
Day 4	30 min
Day 5	20 min
Day 6	Complete rest
Day 7	RACE DAY

Your Triathlon Training Schedule

You'll find some blank triathlon training grids in the back of the book, one for each phase. You can duplicate these grids and fill them in with your personal training schedules. Note: if you need to go through an initiation period in one or two activities, integrate those workouts with your base training in the other(s). If you are new to swimming, biking, and running, you will need to plan a separate workout schedule based entirely on the initiation phase before you can begin base training.

Part III
Tri-ing Your Best

There's a whole lot more to triathlons than just training. Being the best triathlete you can be depends on other important factors. Nutrition, injury prevention, and knowing what to expect for your upcoming race are key variables in your multisport experience. And, finally, figuring out just how triathlon fits into everything else in your life is just as relevant to your success as all that technical know-how.

Chapter 8

Fueling Up for Triathlon

> "If we're not willing to settle for junk living, we certainly shouldn't settle for junk food."
>
> —*Sally Edwards, business woman, author, and Ironman triathlete*

When you think of food, fuel may be the last thing you think about. Yet what you put into your body has an enormous effect on your energy level and, if you're training for triathlons, on performance. Food *is* fuel, but what's the right kind of fuel?

Sports nutrition is a new field that addresses the unique nutritional needs of active people. Nutritional frontiers are being charted every day as competitive triathletes demand more from their bodies and learn about how good nutrition enables them to reach higher levels of performance. But sports nutrition isn't just for competitive triathletes; it's concerned with the dietary needs of active people, such as yourself, who are delving into the challenging activity of triathlon for many reasons, reasons that may have nothing to do with competition.

Proper nutrition means meeting your daily caloric requirement and providing your body with the nutrients it needs for the growth, support, and repair of tissue. That may sound simple, but without some fundamental nutrition knowledge, sports nutrition can be a confusing maze of scientific terminology and theory. To help you better understand the link between eating and triathlon training, this chapter will seek to answer the most commonly asked sports nutrition questions. In doing so, I hope to present the scientific facts without the scientific jargon.

Carbing Up

You've probably heard of carbo-loading, but for many people, there's a shroud of mystery around the process of converting carbohydrates in food into energy. The following sections provide a few facts about carbohydrates to clear things up.

Carbohydrates Are the Best Form of Energy

The energy from food comes in three forms: carbohydrates, protein, and fat. Some of these fuels are stored in your body so that muscles and organs can use them as an immediate source of energy. Foods that you eat just before or during exercise also can fuel muscles.

Out of these three fuels, carbohydrates are the most important nutrient for working muscles. Carbohydrates are the primarily energy source for most forms of physical activity and are burned more efficiently than protein or fat. Research has shown that the energy from carbohydrates can be released within exercising muscles up to three times as fast as the energy from fat.

The primary function of carbohydrates is to provide energy. The drawback is that the body can store a very limited supply of carbohydrates at any given time. Two hours or less of endurance exercise may deplete liver and muscle glycogen (stored carbohydrate) levels. Therefore, a high-carbohydrate diet is essential to perform at your best.

Carbohydrates have other important functions:

- Carbohydrates are the only fuel that the brain and nervous system can use effectively. Low carbohydrate stores may cause diminished concentration.
- Adequate amounts of carbohydrates help spare protein reserves needed for muscle growth, maintenance, and repair.
- Carbohydrates help the body burn fat more efficiently. Scientific literature often states that "fat burns best in a carbohydrate flame."
- Many foods high in carbohydrates (such as whole grains, fruits, and vegetables) are also high in dietary fiber for better digestion and prevention of certain types of cancer.

Carb Intake

The average person's diet should be comprised of at least 60 percent of daily caloric intake from carbohydrates. For example, a person who needs 3,000 calories per day to sustain body weight should eat nearly 2,000 calories from carbohydrates (or 500 grams of carbohydrates) per day.

Triathletes, especially those training for longer events, need more and should shoot for a carbohydrate intake of 65 to 70 percent (more on this later in this chapter). Even if you don't consider yourself a competitive triathlete, food high in carbohydrates should be the foundation of a balanced diet for everyone. A high-carbohydrate diet is vital for anyone who leads an active lifestyle and exercises on a near-daily basis, regardless of whether that person is focused on performance.

Also, glycogen depletion is cumulative; after a few days of eating a low-carbohydrate diet and working out regularly, you may start to feel stale and worn-out. Finally, a low-carbohydrate diet generally means that a large percentage of daily caloric intake will come from high-fat sources. The potential health-related problems of a high-fat diet have been well documented.

In recent years, a flood of sports nutrition products have come out that contain a higher percentage of fat and protein. The basis for these products is a popular theory among some nutrition experts, which many dub as the 40/30/30 formula. These products have a ratio of 40 percent of calories from carbohydrates, 30 percent from protein, and 30 percent from fat. The basic premise is that this ratio helps the body burn fat more efficiently during workouts. A ton of 40/30/30 products geared to endurance athletes have riddled the market, yet most mainstream nutritionists don't endorse the 40/30/30 belief. Until indisputable scientific data can prove these claims, it's best to make carbohydrates your primary source of fuel.

Rice, pasta, breads, cereals, fruits, vegetables, and whole grains are high in carbohydrates. Eating these foods is an excellent way to increase carbohydrate stores in the body. Carbohydrates can be consumed in solid, gel, or liquid form.

Timing Your Carbs

Besides eating a high-carbohydrate diet daily, the timing of meals is important. To maximize the effects of proper nutrition on performance, you need to follow some specific guidelines before, during, and after exercise.

1. Before exercise

   Benefits: Eating carbohydrates before exercise increases muscle glycogen (carbohydrate stores) and helps maintain normal blood sugar levels.

   Guidelines: Consume 75 or more grams of carbohydrates one to two hours before training. For example, one bagel and one cup of pasta have a combined total of 75 grams of carbohydrates.

2. During exercise

   Benefits: During exercise, muscle and liver glycogen stores may become depleted, leading to a drop in blood sugar. This

Racing Tip

Just where do you put those little gel packets or tubes during your bike or run? Well, fortunately, many neat gadgets have surfaced to hold gel products since they've become so popular. Any pro bicycle shop or triathlon race expo will offer everything from tiny holders that clip on to your running shorts waistband to gel flasks that resemble mini water bottles and attach to your bicycle frame. If you decide to carry a gel product with you under a cap or in your hand, make sure you don't litter the race course with empty gel packets.

drop could result in headaches, dizziness, muscle weakness, fatigue, and reduced performance. Consuming carbohydrates during endurance exercise can postpone fatigue and prolong peak performance.

Guidelines: Drink 4 to 10 ounces of a fluid replacement drink, such as Gatorade®, every 15 to 20 minutes during exercise.

3. After exercise

Benefits: After exercise, carbohydrate intake will speed muscle recovery by replenishing glycogen stores. Immediately following exercise is a brief time frame when it is essential to replenish carbohydrates; this time frame is known as the carbohydrate window. Studies have shown that when athletes ate carbohydrates in the hours following endurance exercise, their muscles recovered faster.

Guidelines: Immediately following exercise, and for the next three hours, consume .75 grams of carbohydrates per hour for every pound of body weight. After that, continue eating a high-carbohydrate diet for rapid recovery.

What about that carbo-loading stuff? Carbohydrate-loading, or carbo-loading, is a nutrition strategy designed to increase muscle glycogen capacity in the days before an endurance event by boosting carbohydrate intake and decreasing training. We'll talk about carbo-loading and other race week strategies in greater detail in chapter 10.

Sample High-Carbohydrate Meals

Here's a sampling of some high-carbohydrate meals. When you add it all up, approximately 66 percent of your calories from these meals come from carbohydrates, 17 percent come from protein, and 16 percent come from fat.

Breakfast

4 slices whole-wheat toast

1 tbsp. peanut butter

3/4 cup Grape Nuts® cereal

1 cup skim milk

1 cup strawberries

1 cup orange juice

Lunch

2 oz. lean beef patty

1 whole-grain hamburger bun (with condiments)

1 cup low-fat pasta salad

1 apple

1 cup skim milk

Dinner

3 oz. broiled chicken breast, skinless

1 cup brown rice pilaf

1 slice whole-wheat bread

1 tsp. margarine

1 1/2 cup green salad

1 tomato

1 tbsp. low-fat salad dressing

1 cup skim milk

8 oz. low-fat frozen yogurt

Healthy Snacks (2 to 4 times a day)

1 large pretzel

1 banana

1 bagel (option: low-fat cream cheese)

1 high-carbohydrate energy bar

That Gooey Stuff

One of the biggest-selling sports nutrition products recently introduced into the triathlete market is carbohydrate gels. No, you don't splotch the stuff on your hair to be more aerodynamic. You eat this gooey mess, much like you would an energy bar or any sports supplement.

Gels are essentially sports drinks without the water. They are composed primarily of carbohydrates, though some include very small amounts of protein. A few products throw in some other ingredients: minute amounts of caffeine, herbs, vitamins, and minerals. Gels typically come in small, convenient packets or tubes, which can be easily carried in a bicycle jersey or tucked in the side of your running shorts or under a cap.

The best use of gels is as a racing aid, especially in longer events. If you have stomach problems whenever you eat carbohydrates in the form of solids or sports drinks, you may find gels to be more digestible. Of course, as with anything you intend to try in a race, always test a gel product during a training session. Also, don't substitute gels for fluid intake; you still need to make sure you drink enough during workouts and races.

You may have noticed that since starting triathlon training, your eating habits have changed a bit.

Carbs and Stomach Problems

Because high-carbohydrate foods are usually high in fiber, they fill the stomach and make you feel full, sometimes causing stomach distress or, possibly, excessive gas. If you experience these symptoms because of a high-carbohydrate diet, try eating more frequently than three meals a day. Consuming several high-carbohydrate snacks throughout the day, such as bagels, fruit, rice cakes, and butterless popcorn, may make it easier to meet your carbohydrate needs.

Another solution may be to consume a carbohydrate-loading and recovery drink. These drinks are specifically formulated for before or after exercise, or as a supplement to help boost daily carb intake. Active people and athletes sometimes find it difficult to consume a diet high in carbohydrates, especially because many of these foods contain a significant amount of fiber. The carbo-loading drinks are a convenient way to ingest large amounts of carbohydrates, without having to ingest enormous quantities of filling foods. However, your diet should not consist of a majority of these beverages; you need the complex carbs of nutritious foods such as fruits, vegetables, and grains.

The balance you get in your diet from eating a variety of foods high in carbohydrates and other nutrients is important too. Unfortunately, balanced nutrition is often a low priority for many active people, and seldom is it possible to eat the perfect diet in today's hectic society. Some sports nutrition products contain a good balance of calories from carbohydrates, protein, and fat and are fortified with vitamins and minerals to help supplement the weak spots in your diet. (There is more on sports nutrition products later in the chapter.)

Choosing Energy Bars

Energy bars have become very popular in recent years, and can be a reliable source of carbohydrates and balanced nutrition. But you have to choose your bar carefully; many products make impressive claims that are without scientific basis. Some energy bars are high in fat and contain partially hydrogenated oils and other ingredients that are not nutritious. If in doubt, check the food label on the wrapper.

After you've checked the food label of a handful of different candidates, try each of them as a healthy snack during the day to evaluate for taste. This testing may take a while, because some brands have a wide variety of flavors. It's important to find one that makes your unique taste buds tingle. If you're not inclined to eat it while you're standing still, chances are that energy bar that tastes like a piece of rubber to you won't be eaten during a long run either.

Dispelling the Protein Myth

Protein is perhaps the most misunderstood nutrient. It's ironic that although many people worry about not getting enough of it, most Americans surpass the recommended daily intake of protein. For triathletes, studies have found that protein does play a role in faster recovery.

Protein's Role

The principal role of protein is to build and repair body tissues, including muscles, ligaments, and tendons. Protein also plays a part in the production of enzymes and hormones, thus serving a regulatory function. Contrary to popular belief, protein is not a primary source of energy, even for athletes engaged in heavy training.

Protein can be used for energy, but it must first be converted to carbohydrates or fat. During the latter stages of an endurance event, such as a long-distance triathlon, when glycogen stores are depleted, protein can supply up to 15 percent of the calories burned (but if calorie and carbohydrate intake are adequate, protein usage could be much lower).

Protein and Amino Acids

Proteins are composed of individual units called amino acids. There are 20 different amino acids, 11 of which are produced by the body. The other nine are called essential amino acids and must be obtained from the foods we eat. If essential amino acids are not consumed, the body's ability to produce certain proteins will be impaired, and health and performance may suffer. The typical American diet usually supplies all the essential amino acids. Although there are many claims that amino acid supplements enhance muscle growth and physical performance, there is little sound scientific evidence to support these claims.

Your Protein Needs

The typical American diet contains 200 to 250 percent of the recommended daily intake of protein. So even if you think you need to double your consumption of protein, chances are pretty good that your diet already provides adequate protein. As a good rule of thumb, protein should comprise about 15 percent of your daily caloric intake.

Some studies have confirmed that a small to moderate amount of protein intake after a long workout or race can help speed muscle recovery. A number of sports supplements have added protein to their products for this reason. An energy bar with a moderate amount of protein (10 to 20 grams) and a high-carbohydrate drink is a good post-exercise meal.

The Fear of Fat

Oooh, the "F" word. Fat is perhaps the most feared of nutrients, yet it does play a significant role in a triathlete's diet. Besides providing a stored form of energy, fat contributes to healthy skin and is part of the structure of many hormones and cell membranes. Fat also allows fat-soluble vitamins, such as A, D, E, and K, to be absorbed by your body. Although most people abhor the fat stored on their bodies, fat cushions and protects delicate internal organs, such as the kidneys and liver. Fat even performs a life-saving function by helping the body form blood clots to stop bleeding.

Too Much of a Good Thing

Overconsumption of fat poses two major problems. First, fat is a very concentrated source of energy, so small amounts of it provide many calories and can lead to weight gain and obesity. Second, a high-fat diet can lead to the development of heart disease and certain types of cancer. Chronic diseases related to high fat intake are associated with two of the ten leading causes of death in the United States. Most nutrition authorities promote a reduction of fat in the American diet from the current 40 to 45 percent to fewer than 30 percent of total calories from fat.

Though current FDA guidelines recommend that 30 percent of daily calories come from fat, triathletes may wish to lower their fat intake to 20 percent or less of their caloric intake so that a greater portion of their calories come from carbohydrates. But even triathletes need some fat in their diet to perform vital functions and promote the absorption of fat-soluble vitamins. Female triathletes with below normal body fat are likely to experience a disruption in their menstrual cycle and a related loss of calcium, making them more prone to stress fractures.

What You Can Do to Reduce Fat in Your Diet

Eating healthy shouldn't mean a drastic crash-course diet, but rather a sustained effort over time to make intelligent choices:

- Watch out for hidden fat. Sweet foods such as bran muffins, donuts, cookies, cakes, and pies have more fat than sugar calories. Similarly, crackers, chips, and other snack foods are high in fat. If in doubt, read the food labels.
- Cut down on the sauces and toppings added to your food. Gravy, salad dressing, sour cream, butter, margarine, mayonnaise, and whipped cream are almost all fat. Even small amounts of these foods can boost the fat content of your diet.
- Buy low-fat dairy products. Skim milk has the same nutritional value as whole milk, but no fat and half the calories. Cottage cheese, yogurt, and frozen yogurt made from skim milk have this same advantage.
- Use low-fat cooking techniques such as broiling, grilling, and stir-frying, rather than deep-frying or pan-frying. If you eat out, ask how the food is prepared before ordering.
- Select lean cuts of meat, such as loin or round. The grade of meat is based on the fat content. Choice and prime grade are the highest in fat; the less-expensive select grade is the lowest in fat.
- Remove the visible fat from meat before cooking it and drain the grease from hamburger after frying it. Also, before eating poultry, remove the skin.

Making Healthy Food Choices

Committing to healthy eating should be a corollary commitment to training for multisport events. Reading and correctly interpreting the new food labels and the Food Guide Pyramid are two ways to become more aware of what you're putting in your mouth.

Reading Food Labels

To help the American consumer better understand the contents of foods and make better dietary choices, the Food and Drug Adminis-

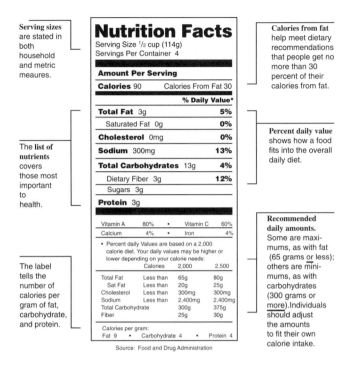

Serving sizes are stated in both household and metric meaures.

The list of nutrients covers those most important to health.

The label tells the number of calories per gram of fat, carbohydrate, and protein.

Nutrition Facts

Serving Size ¹/₂ cup (114g)
Servings Per Container 4

Amount Per Serving

Calories 90   Calories From Fat 30

% Daily Value*

Total Fat 3g	**5%**
Saturated Fat 0g	**0%**
Cholesterol 0mg	**0%**
Sodium 300mg	**13%**
Total Carbohydrates 13g	**4%**
Dietary Fiber 3g	**12%**
Sugars 3g	
Protein 3g	

Vitamin A	80%	Vitamin C	60%
Calcium	4%	Iron	4%

* Percent daily Values are based on a 2,000 calorie diet. Your daily values may be higher or lower depending on your calorie needs:

		Calories	2,000	2,500
Total Fat	Less than		65g	80g
Sat Fat	Less than		20g	25g
Cholesterol	Less than		300mg	300mg
Sodium	Less than		2,400mg	2,400mg
Total Carbohydrate			300g	375g
Fiber			25g	30g

Calories per gram:
Fat 9   •   Carbohydrate 4   •   Protein 4

Source: Food and Drug Administration

Calories from fat help meet dietary recommendations that people get no more than 30 percent of their calories from fat.

Percent daily value shows how a food fits into the overall daily diet.

Recommended daily amounts. Some are maximums, as with fat (65 grams or less); others are minimums, as with carbohydrates (300 grams or more).Individuals should adjust the amounts to fit their own calorie intake.

A typical food label.

tration redesigned the label format for packaged foods (see above). The new label is also structured to help the individual with health problems limit their intake of certain nutrients—fat, sugar, or salt, for instance—or increase their consumption of others, such as fiber or calcium.

The new food label is a good way to determine the nutritional value of packaged foods and is a general guideline for eating a healthy diet. But the triathletes must make several modifications when reading food labels:

- The Daily Values tell you how much of a day's recommended total allotment of nutrients is contained in the food. The percents of Daily Values are based on a 2,000-calorie diet, which is usually lower than the number of calories a physically active person needs to maintain weight and ingest the required amounts of nutrients. A better method is to calculate the grams of carbohydrates you need daily and aim for that amount.

- The Daily Values are based on a diet comprised of 60 percent of calories from carbohydrates. Athletes who need to replace glycogen stores depleted during exercise may wish to increase carbohydrate intake to 65 percent of their daily diet. For example, the athlete on a 3,500-calorie diet should consume 570 grams of carbohydrates daily.

- If you stick to the Daily Values, your daily caloric intake of fat will be 30 percent, a good target. But the health-conscious person may wish to aim for a better target of 20 percent of daily caloric intake from fat.

- The bottom section of the food label lists the recommended daily intake of nutrients for a 2,000- and 2,500-calorie diet. As a triathlete, you may have higher caloric needs, more often in the 3,000 to 3,500 range, and closer to 5,000 for athletes training for ultra-endurance events, such as an Ironman distance triathlon. Accordingly, nutrient requirements will be much higher.

- You may also want to use the maximum grams of fat recommended per day as a range. Thus, if you aim for a daily fat intake of 65 to 80 grams per day while increasing your recommended carbohydrate consumption, your diet will be better suited for the rigorous nutritional demands of exercise.

The Food Guide Pyramid

Like the outdated Four Food Groups graphic, the new Food Guide Pyramid (see next page) is a guide for a healthy diet. It calls for eating a variety of foods to get the nutrients you need and the right amount of calories to maintain healthy weight. But it was created as a guide for the general population, which as a whole, does not exercise as much as you probably do (or will). As an active triathlete, your needs might be slightly different.

Here are a few slight modifications to consider:

- Triathletes in training need more calories than the recommended servings. Modify the recommendations by snacking on foods high in carbohydrates and low in fat between and with meals.

- For the triathlete burning a substantial amount of calories in training, increase the number of servings on the first and second levels of the Pyramid.

- The servings recommended by the USDA are somewhat low in calories, ranging between 250 to 375 calories per serving.

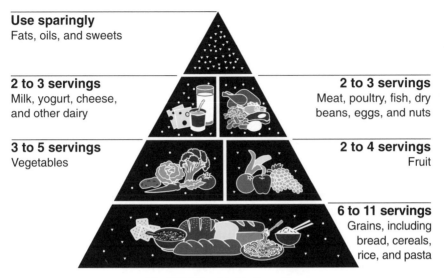

Use sparingly
Fats, oils, and sweets

2 to 3 servings
Milk, yogurt, cheese,
and other dairy

2 to 3 servings
Meat, poultry, fish, dry
beans, eggs, and nuts

3 to 5 servings
Vegetables

2 to 4 servings
Fruit

6 to 11 servings
Grains, including
bread, cereals,
rice, and pasta

The USDA Food Guide Pyramid.

Another way to get the calories you need as an active person is to increase the serving size.

- Triathletes need to be especially concerned about replenishing glycogen stores during long or intense training or competition. To meet their unique nutritional needs during exercise, triathletes should consume fluid-replacement drinks and other products designed for use during exercise.

Vitamins and Supplements

When you get involved in triathlon and start reading the magazines, you're sure to notice the plethora of "magic bullet" supplements out there. They'll promise everything from increased endurance to faster times. But do they really work? Although these products may provide some performance benefits, most nutritionists agree that a healthy diet is far more beneficial to your triathlon training than anything you'll find in a pill (no matter how many advertising dollars are spent trying to convince you otherwise). Bottom line: a balanced and nutritious diet high in whole foods and complex carbohydrates is the cornerstone of good nutrition and should provide you with all the vitamins and minerals you need. However, some people take supplements to compensate for poor eating habits.

Karl's Diet Dilemma

The first few years of triathlon racing for Karl Hausmann went pretty well. He did his first race in 1990 and, when he realized he had a talent for speed, started actively competing in his age group in 1993. But for the next few years, he experienced symptoms such as dizziness, upper respiratory problems, unusual fatigue, and slow recovery from workouts. Doctors found an alarmingly low red blood cell count and an almost nonexistent level of iron in his body.

"After a few years of racing hard on the average person's diet, my body was beat up pretty good," says the 28-year-old small business consultant living in Austin, Texas. "It took a lot of testing and a period of iron supplementation to get things back to normal. I learned that I needed much more in terms of nutrients than the average person."

With a more balanced diet that contains more of the nutrients he needs, including natural fat and protein, Karl has licked his diet dilemma. He has since garnered several age group wins and qualified for the Hawaiian Ironman, and his racing has returned to optimum form, so much so that he plans to race professionally in 1998. "My advice to newcomers to the sport is to pay special attention to your body's warning signs and to realize that you need more of everything—more nutrients, more calories, more fluids—if you're going to be training hard," says Karl.

Taken to an extreme, some supplements may even be harmful to you. Fat-soluble vitamins (A, D, E, and K) are stored in the body and can build up to toxic levels if taken in excessive amounts. If you think your diet is not quite up to par, your best bet is a multivitamin with moderate amounts of essential nutrients.

The Fluid Facts

We've touched upon the importance of fluids previously, but this is such a vital area of concern for triathletes that it's worth taking a closer look. Water is our most essential nutrient; we can live longer without food than we can without water. Water comprises 60 percent of our body weight, and blood is 90 percent water. Lost fluids need to be replaced regularly throughout the day to maintain proper body temperature and energy-producing capabilities.

The body keeps cool during exercise by circulating blood to the skin, where water is lost in the form of sweat. Eventually, if you lose enough water, you'll put undue strain on your cardiovascular system, causing performance to deteriorate. In extreme cases, dehydration can lead to heart failure, among other things, and death can occur.

Most active people have experienced mild dehydration without knowing it. This is because the signs of mild dehydration can be subtle. To improve your performance, tune in to your body's signals of dehydration:

- Fatigue
- Loss of appetite
- Flushed skin
- Heat intolerance
- Light-headedness
- Small amount of dark yellow urine

What You Need

An average, nonexercising adult needs about two quarts of fluids per day to replace normal water loss. Triathletes training for a multisport event obviously need more. To evaluate your fluid needs, weigh yourself before and after each workout. Every pound you lose equals approximately two cups of fluid. Drink enough fluids to compensate for any weight loss, plus your normal daily requirement of two quarts.

For particularly hard workouts on very hot days, follow these guidelines:

- Before exercising, drink one to two cups of fluid.
- During exercise, drink four to six ounces of water or a fluid-replacement drink every 15 to 20 minutes.
- After exercise, drink plenty of fluids, even if you aren't thirsty (thirst is a poor indicator of fluid needs).

Types of Sports Drinks

So far I've used the term "sports drink" to mean products designed to be used for exercise. But there are many different kinds of sports nutrition products, each with its own formulation and purpose. If you add gels and energy bars to the list of choices, things can get pretty confusing.

To help clarify your choices, following are brief descriptions of the three major categories of sports drinks available to you today (naming brands doesn't imply endorsement—it just makes it easier to illustrate the distinctions between types). Also, new sports nutrition products are being introduced constantly, so if you don't understand their use, read the label carefully or contact the manufacturer. At the end of this chapter, you'll also find a usage chart that sums up your sports nutrition choices.

Fluid-Replacement Drinks

Fluid-replacement drinks help replace fluids, carbohydrates, and vital nutrients lost during exercise. Usually, these drinks are somewhat sweet, from mild to strong, depending on the brand and flavor. They contain glucose, fructose, or a glucose polymer, or in many cases, they combine these ingredients as a carbohydrate source. They may also contain nutrients, such as potassium and sodium, which are depleted during exercise. Brands include Gatorade®, Powerade®, Allsport® , Cytomax®, and Hydra Fuel®.

Carbo-Loading or Recovery Drinks

These beverages are for use before or after exercise or as a supplement for use when you are carbo-loading. They typically contain a similar carbohydrate source as their fluid-replacement counterparts, but they have more of it. For example, although the carbohydrate potency of most fluid-replacement drinks falls in the 6 to 8 percent range, carbo-loading and recovery drinks can be as strong as 20 percent or more.

So does that mean more carbohydrates are better, and that, because this stuff is stronger, you should be using it during exercise? In this case, more is definitely *not* better. During exercise, you need something that will digest easily and be absorbed into your bloodstream quickly. Researchers have found that a 6- to 8-percent carbohydrate solution works best to accomplish this during exercise. The high carbs of recovery drinks will help you recover faster from the workout, and the stronger solution shouldn't upset your stomach when you are not exercising. Brands include GatorLode® and Ultra Fuel®.

Balanced Nutrition Shakes

Sometimes referred to as "sports shakes," these drinks are typically dairy or dairy-like and include important nutrients without the bulk.

They contain mostly carbohydrates, a moderate amount of protein, a small amount of fat, and are often packed with vitamins and minerals. Several products are even lactose-free, reducing the risk of nausea in lactose-intolerant athletes.

Balanced nutrition shakes are great for people who have a hard time eating right. They make a quick, healthy, snack, pre-event meal, or recovery drink. Brands include GatorPro®, Endura Optimizer®,

Choosing a Fluid-Replacement Drink

You now know that fluid-replacement drinks can supply you with vital fluids, carbohydrates for energy, and vital nutrients such as sodium and potassium. But out of all the available brands, how do you choose the one that's right for you? These tips may help:

- Avoid carbonated drinks, which can cause gastrointestinal distress. This distress, in turn, will likely cause you to drink less fluid, which may lead to dehydration.

- Avoid beverages containing alcohol or caffeine. They are diuretics and tend to contribute to fluid loss.

- Choose a fluid-replacement beverage that tastes good. If it doesn't have a pleasant taste, you're not likely to drink enough of it.

- Choose a drink with a carbohydrate concentration of 6 to 8 percent. Studies have shown that this is the optimum range and is absorbed from the intestine significantly faster than anything over an 8-percent concentration and 30 percent faster than water.

and Metabolol II®. In the mainstream market, products such as Ensure® and Boost®, are often very similar.

Your SportsNutrition Choices

Table 8.1 may help clarify some of the product choices triathletes have nowadays. As you'll see, there is a lot of crossover usage between products. For example, a fluid-replacement drink, such as Gatorade®, is primarily designed for use during exercise, but there's certainly no harm in having some before exercise, after exercise, or at anytime during the day. An energy bar is good just about anytime as well, but shouldn't be eaten during a race unless it's been tested under training conditions for digestibility.

The large checkmarks in the chart denote the product's primary uses; the smaller ones represent secondary uses. If an area is not marked, the product should not be used for this purpose. Also, remember that a "Before" designation means that these products should be consumed one to two hours before exercise to allow for digestion.

Table 8.1 Sports Nutrition Product Usage Chart

	Before exercise	During exercise	After exercise	Anytime
Fluid-replacement drinks	Ⓥ	✔	Ⓥ	Ⓥ
Carbo-loading/recovery drinks	✔		✔	Ⓥ
Balanced nutrition shakes	✔		✔	✔
Energy bars	✔	Ⓥ	✔	✔
Carbohydrate gels	Ⓥ	✔	Ⓥ	Ⓥ

Note: For training and racing longer than the Olympic distance, energy bars can be used during exercise.

✔ = Primary use

Ⓥ = Secondary use

Chapter 9

Staying Healthy

> "Sometimes the most urgent and vital thing you can do is take a complete rest."
>
> —*Ashleight Brilliant*

In the late 1970s when thousands took to running marathons, a large portion of these enthusiastic masses, ignorant of proper training practices and the wisdom of increasing mileage safely, were plagued with overuse and trauma injuries. To add insult to injury (literally), few in the traditional medical community had expertise in sports medicine. So if you went to your doctor, he or she would have probably told you to stop running. (The late Dr. George Sheehan said at the time: "The jogger has three natural enemies: drivers, dogs, and doctors.")

Many triathletes come from running backgrounds, and you may have your own tales of injury battles won and lost. You probably know that the natural benefit of cross-training is a lower susceptibility to injury, and perhaps that's one of the major factors that helped you make the decision to jump into multisports.

Sports injuries are most often caused by overuse. A key word to remember when you feel like throwing common sense out the window during training is *moderation*. Moderation comes from the Latin word *moderatus*, which mean to limit extremes. The focus of the first part of this chapter is steering clear of injuries and the overtraining that leads to them. But if you've already been injured, or at sometime in the future need to know more about an injury, I've also provided an overview of the six injuries most common to triathletes, as well as some recovery, training adjustment, and prevention tips.

Preventing Injuries

Although fitness and health may seem synonymous, many marathoners have ruined their knees by putting in way too much mileage in too short a period of time. Sure, their heart rates may be phenomenal—maybe 40 or 44 beats per minute, which indicates a strong, efficient cardiovascular system. But they're hobbling around on a damaged joint because at some point they sacrificed their health in an effort to attain fitness.

"Most triathletes are not pros. They participate as part of a lifestyle," says Dr. Daryll Hobson, physician to professional triathletes like Mark Allen. "They enter the sport with the idea that if I'm fit, I'm going to be healthy, which is a mistake. In striving for fitness, they often destroy their health. Many triathletes tend to want to get someplace very quickly too. They're not willing to do the work of establishing a high level of fitness performance and maintaining health simultaneously."

The Importance of Rest

It may sound rather simplistic, but most injuries can be avoided by simply building enough rest into a training program. As you learned in the chapters on training, rest is a key component of any good triathlon regimen. Yet rest is perhaps the hardest thing for a competitive triathlete to do. That may sound ironic, but one look at the number of articles and books written on sports injuries clearly shows that athletes and physically active people have a hard time dealing with rest.

Runners are particularly notorious for overdoing it. In *The Runner's Complete Medical Guide*, the authors address the irony of running injuries: "Runners are the fittest group of sick and injured people in the world. While running is probably the most natural and healthful sport ever played, its participants most frequently push their mental and physical capacities to the limit."

Most sports injuries are a result of not allowing the body enough rest and recovery time. Planning and following a smart and effective training schedule that builds in rest days and easy training days for recovery is crucial to avoiding injury. But even if you do that, there's still a possibility that you need a long period of rest, especially if you've gone berserk and have been training hard and racing just about every weekend (not uncommon for overzealous newcomers to the sport).

Forcing yourself to take a long rest is particularly important if you've been training for and just completed a full triathlon season in a part of the country that enjoys good weather year-round and holds plenty of multisport events within driving distance. In many subtle ways, the long months of training have taken their toll on your body and maybe on your mind. (Can you spell B-U-R-N-O-U-T?)

The problem is that many triathletes are bundles of nervous energy when it comes to rest. Triathlon can become an addiction,

Milo never, ever missed a workout.

albeit a healthy addiction. Without the soothing effect of the exercise high, many triathletes find it difficult to take a rest day or build an easy swim, bike ride, or run workout into a training schedule.

Listening to Your Body

Just how do you know when to take an easy day or maybe even a day or two off from training altogether? World-class athletes learn to monitor their internal workings, to be in tune with any—however slight—indication of pending injury. When a professional endurance athlete feels he or she is pushing that fine red line of human performance, he or she knows that injury may be just around the corner.

Endurance training makes the constant monitoring of bodily processes an absolute necessity. "Listen to your body" becomes a divine commandment when applied to training. Injury is the price paid for disobedience. Most experts concur that body awareness affects the ability of an athlete to avoid overtraining. Yet, with all the internal variables (not to mention external variables such as bike fit, technique, equipment, and so on), how can you go about establishing a body awareness as keen as that of a trained professional? How do you know when you're pushing that human stress gauge to the maximum?

When Training Leads to Unhealthy Stress

When you train, a certain amount of stress is normal. But once you begin to overtrain, unhealthy stress and the symptoms that go along with it often precede injury.

Perhaps the best opportunity to monitor your stress level is the sympathetic nervous system. This system mediates the response of the body to stress, playing a major role in speeding up heart rate, increasing blood pressure, and mobilizing energy reserves. Forty years of research by stress researcher and renowned expert Hans Selye on the sympathetic nervous system shows that there is a point in the human body when a healthy stress level can become unhealthy stress. Dr. Hobson, a big believer in Hans Selye's research, contends that there are signs of an overstressed body. Look upon them as the body's natural meter gauge with a well-defined red line.

Possible Signs of Overtraining

Although these symptoms may be indications of possible forthcoming injury, only experience will draw out the strongest, most dependable warning signs that determine whether you're training too hard. The warning signs that can foretell pending injury for one person may be false alarms for others. For example, I often experience sugar cravings, eye strain, and moodiness when I overtrain, but rarely have the other symptoms listed here.

- A strong craving for sugar on rest days
- Inconsistent episodes of blurred vision and a feeling of eye strain and sensitivity
- Varying degrees of joint pain, particularly in the vulnerable sacroiliac (lower back) and knee
- Muscle weakness, particularly in the calf and medial (inside) of knee
- Getting sick easily with slow recovery
- Allergic reactions (more than usual)

- Insomnia or an inability to relax and subsequent loss of sleep
- Poor digestion
- Excessive nervousness and irritability
- Lack of energy with no reserve energy to surge in the latter half of a workout
- Episodes of dizziness when standing up from a lying or squatting position

An Injury-Free Pigg

Professional triathlete Mike Pigg had a reputation early on in the sport as a "go 'till you drop" lunatic case, but he has mellowed considerably in the latter portion of his professional career. Once a paying member of the "Overtraining Club," Mike has changed his ways and his lifestyle. As a result, he has successfully avoided any serious sports injuries in recent years.

"Now I train in an environment where there's no peer pressure," says Mike, who has been competing for over 13 years. "I'm not in a swimming pool with a bunch of guys calling me a wimp if I don't do another 1,000. If I feel pain in my shoulder, I just take a day off."

Mike has, at times, experienced minor lower back problems, especially early in the season. The constant strain and twisting during long bike rides often takes a toll on any triathlete in the beginning of the season. Several years ago, however, Mike kicked his early-season backaches. His solution? A chain saw. "I had to clear about 30 trees for this property I bought, and I lugged this big chain saw around. I guess it was sort of like a strength-training program in the woods. My back felt great when I started training on the bike."

Mike has two prevention tips: "Be fully confident in your body's ability to let you know when something's wrong. And always do a proper warm-up so your body can gradually adjust to the exercise."

Tips on Getting Back to Health

If you're currently experiencing overtraining, here are some concrete steps you can take to get back on track:

- **Get reacquainted.** There are only so many hours in the day, and if you're like many triathletes trying to make a living and train too, swimming, biking, and running take up a large portion of your free time. If, as a result, you haven't stayed in touch with family or friends, now is the perfect time to make it up to them.

- **Catch up on sleep.** Has your training schedule wreaked havoc with your sleeping pattern? Have you had to get up an hour earlier to get in that run during the week before going to work? Sleep deprivation is cumulative; if you've found your body slow to recover from long or hard runs, the cause could be months of not getting enough sleep. Give yourself a break and allow yourself the proper amount of sleep (whatever that may be—it's different for everyone).

- **Get away from it all.** One of the best ways to recover is to plan a getaway. You don't have to take a week off; even a weekend trip within driving distance can do wonders to rejuvenate your body and mind.

- **Get a massage.** If you can't afford the time or cost of a weekend vacation, you might want to try a nice, relaxing massage. The right kind of massage can speed the recovery process, especially for overuse injuries. It helps improve the blood supply to muscles, improves circulation, and speeds healing.

- **Cut your mileage.** If you just can't bear to be away from running, at the very least, cut down your mileage significantly for a few weeks or even months. If you've been doing any speedwork, such as intervals on the track, give your body a break from these very difficult workouts. If you've been doing some hard hill workouts, cut down or eliminate those from your program as well.

Stretching for Health

As a whole, we triathletes tend to be a very tight group. If we aren't grabbing our Achilles tendons in pain, we're probably massaging

Racing Tip

The goal on race day is not just to be able to complete your event, but to be fit *and* healthy when you cross the finish line. If you've properly trained and tapered, you should feel fresh and energetic, with no muscle aches or soreness. During a race, don't throw your careful attention to health out the window. Listen to your body and any warning signs indicating you're pushing too hard. Don't be afraid to seek medical attention on the race course if you start to feel severe pain, dizziness, or debilitated in any way.

our aching hamstrings from yesterday's track workout. Ironically, we tend to be a very lazy group when it comes to stretching.

Stretching Benefits

If you're like me, you'd rather just jump into your running shoes and head out on the trails before the sun goes down. Besides, let's admit it, stretching isn't the most exciting thing to do. But perhaps a quick review of the benefits derived from greater flexibility might help you look at stretching in a whole new way:

• **Improved performance.** The most attractive benefit of stretching for the triathlete is the improved physical performance. The more flexible a joint, the greater ability it has to move through a bigger range of motion and thus function more efficiently. Recent research at the Human Performance Laboratory at Boise State University showed that 20 minutes of stretching three times a week can increase range of motion by 30 percent.

More specifically, stretching increases the ability of muscle fibers to generate force despite accumulation of lactic acid. Because muscle fibers act by contracting, the longer they are to begin with, the more they are able to contract. Optimum flexibility is accomplished when normal muscle fiber is as long as possible so that when it does inevitably shorten with the introduction of lactic acid into the system, as during prolonged exercise, it is still able to function efficiently.

• **Injury prevention.** Exercise physiologists generally agree that greater flexibility and, hence, greater range of motion makes a person less likely to injure himself. Also, stretching before exercise helps to warm muscles and introduce your body to each workout more gradually so that the possibility of injuries due to working cold muscles too hard without a proper warm-up is decreased. Cold

Stretching shouldn't hurt. Be gentle with yourself and stretch only until you feel a slight discomfort.

muscles are less elastic, making them less capable of moving through a full range of motion, which may lead to strains or tears.

• **Improved coordination.** Greater flexibility increases neuromuscular coordination. It has been shown that the speed of nerve impulses is enhanced with stretching. The central nervous system becomes more sensitive to the physical demands placed on it, so opposing muscle groups work in a more coordinated way.

• **Greater joint elasticity.** Stretching results in greater circulation to the joints. Stretching increases the temperature of the tissue, which in turn increases the blood supply and nutrients to the joint structure. This process promotes greater elasticity in the surrounding tissue.

• **Better posture and movement.** Stretching improves muscular balance and awareness. Stretching helps to realign soft tissue structures, which may have developed poorly through a lifetime of poor posture or normal wear and tear. Realigning tissue structures helps promote and maintain good posture and healthy movement in daily activities and better form in running.

- **Decreased back pain.** There is a decrease in the incidence of lower back pain in those who stretch regularly. The American Council on Exercise indicates that there is strong clinical evidence to show that lumbar-pelvic flexibility, including hamstrings, hip flexors, and muscles attaching to the pelvis, is critical in decreasing stress to the lumbar spine.
- **Relieved muscle tension.** Stretching can relieve muscle tension. When muscles are tense for long periods of time (like during long endurance running), the flow of oxygen to these muscles can be cut off. The result is a buildup of lactic acid in tissues, causing fatigue and muscle tightness or knotting. Stretching can help break up those muscle knots and release lactic acid into the bloodstream.

The Stretching Question

If you've read running books and subscribed to *Runner's World* or any other running publication, chances are you've come across a lot of material on stretching. There are about as many stretching techniques and exercises for runners and triathletes as there are sports drinks. The optimum stretching technique has always been—and will probably always be—a matter of controversy.

However, the type of stretching technique most sports therapists recommend is called static stretching. This conservative technique, traditionally accepted as safe and effective, involves slow elongation through a full range of motion to a point of slight discomfort. This type of stretching has been found to produce long-term gains that are maintained in people who practice consistently. Static stretching is low-intensity and imposes less microtrauma to the tissue, resulting in better flexibility without the element of danger that exists with more radical (and painful) stretching techniques.

Specific stretching instructions and illustrations are beyond the scope of this book. However, most running books cover the fundamental stretches and swimming, cycling, running, and triathlon magazines cover stretching exercises on a regular basis. Concentrate on those exercises that stretch muscle groups that are consistently tight or weak.

Taking Care of Your Feet

By far, running causes the most injuries to triathletes. Of all the things that you can do to prevent running injuries, caring for your feet is perhaps the most crucial. If you think about it, your poor feet take the brunt of the pounding as they propel you over unforgiving surfaces. The fact that these 52 oddly shaped bones kind of crunched together inside a couple of little skin bags can handle all that stress is rather remarkable.

If you've been running for some time, you've probably already had your share of foot pains. Perhaps they've been caused by something as simple as not checking that your socks are neither too thick nor too loose. (This simple precaution will prevent bunching or looseness in your shoes, which often leads to blisters or irritation.) Maybe you rushed through your running shoe purchase or got bad advice from a salesperson and are running in the wrong shoe.

No matter how your foot woes may have originated, avoiding most problems takes just a little effort. Whether foot problems are a

A member of Team Three Amigos prepares for a bike ride on his trusted *Caballo*.

commonplace occurrence or a rarity for you, most conditions can be avoided with some TLC and common sense, not only in the running store, but at home and on the road. The following foot care tips are provided by Dr. Tsatsos, a sports physician with a specialty in podiatry:

- Avoid irregular terrain, such as areas of mud and sand, or poorly maintained trails.
- Wear a sock that wicks away moisture, such as polypropelene or wool.
- Change your socks twice a day.
- If you have two pairs of running shoes, alternate the two so that one is always drying. This will decrease the possibility of athlete's foot.
- Use an antifungal powder. Make sure you cover the areas between the toes.

The Six Injuries Most Common to Triathletes (and How to Avoid Them)

Hopefully, you're too new to the sport to have experienced serious injury. Perhaps the best way for you to avoid any of the following common injuries in your triathlon future is to simply be aware of them. But just in case you have already gotten yourself in a mess, I'll cover some recovery tips, as well as training adjustments you can make. I've talked to several experts in the field of sports medicine, but no chapter in a book can replace a proper diagnosis and the expert treatment advice you'll get from a physician specializing in sports injuries. With that in mind, let's start from the top.

Rotator Cuff Tendinitis (or Tear)

"Swimmer's shoulder" is a general term often used to describe many types of shoulder problems such as muscle strains, pulls, and tendinitis. Rotator cuff tendinitis is frequently caused by pool workouts that are either too much or too hard, an imbalance in shoulder muscles, or poor stroke form. Inflammation occurs due to microscopic muscle tears and stress on the four major shoulder muscles that run together, known as the rotator cuff. Pain is usually localized (confined to that area) though it may radiate down the arm. Stiffness and difficulty extending your arm at a 90-degree angle, weakness when lifting the arm, and pain at night are indications of rotator cuff tendinitis.

Recovery

For minor cases, rest, ice, and compression of the shoulder with an elastic wrap will help reduce pain. In severe cases, an orthopedic surgeon may recommend arthroscopic surgery.

Training Adjustments

Unfortunately, the healing process for this injury is slow because of the poor blood supply in the area. Repetitive activities that cause you to extend your arm will increase the inflammation and the risk of a tear. Therefore, unless your case is minor, your sports physician will probably want you to put any swimming or upper body weight training workouts on hold until the shoulder is healthy. Depending on your position, the injury may be aggravated on the bicycle. Sitting upright on a windtrainer or indoor bicycle machine without taking your shoulder to a 90-degree angle is a good alternative exercise.

Prevention Tips

Don't increase your distance or interval workout in the pool too quickly. Work on developing balanced strength in your shoulders by weight training of your biceps, deltoids, pectorals, and trapezius muscles.

SI Dysfunction (Lower Back Pain)

The sacroiliac joint (SI) is a major joint in the body connecting the back and the hip. Unlike other joints surrounded by muscle, the SI relies predominantly on ligaments for support. When these ligaments become irritated, either by a structural or muscle imbalance, the term SI dysfunction is often used to describe this sports injury. The pain is usually located in the lower back area, just above the hip, and is a dull ache, but it can become sharp if training continues. Sometimes the pain may radiate to other areas of the back and hip.

"I prefer to use the term pelvic twist," says Dr. P. Michael Leahy, advisor to the American Chiropractic Association's Council on Sports Injury and Physical Fitness. "The SI is not the only thing involved. You have to look at muscle weakness or structural problems; sometimes it's both." Several years ago, Dr. Leahy compiled statistics on common injuries to triathletes at the '93 Ironman Triathlon in Hawaii. He found SI dysfunction to be one of the three injuries most common to multisport athletes.

Recovery

Because of the poor blood supply to ligaments in the lower back, the road to complete recovery can take some time, but Leahy estimates that one-third of lower back injuries can be attributed to structural imbalances, thus requiring relatively simple treatment. Studies have shown that chiropractic manipulation, in conjunction with back stretching and strengthening exercise, can be very effective.

Training Adjustments

Lower back problems can occur in and be affected by many sports, which makes any training extremely difficult. If your case is mild and is not aggravated by swimming, your sports physician may allow some low-level workouts. Once the pain has subsided and your doctor gives you the green light, gradually work your way back to your normal routine.

Prevention Tips

Locate and correct any structural imbalances in your running or cycling motion (such as those caused by leg length discrepancy). A certified sports medicine physician should be able to help you locate imbalances and suggest ways to correct them or limit their impact on you. Check your aero position on the bicycle—is it uncomfortable and causing you back pain? If so, better to sacrifice a little aerodynamics for greater comfort and health. Also, identify and strengthen any weak muscles that may cause lower back problems. By implementing a lower back stretching and strengthening regimen when you're healthy, you'll avoid most back problems.

Hamstring Muscle Tear

A hamstring muscle tear is a condition that may occur suddenly while you are running or cycling, particularly during an intense session, such as an interval workout or a finish line sprint. Downhill running is another possible cause. The tear is usually caused by tight hamstrings, often due to overtraining or muscle imbalance. Hamstring muscle tears often occur at the tendons near the knee or hip, though a tear in the central portion of the hamstring is not uncommon. The pain is usually sharp and located in a very specific area. Muscle spasms may occur as well.

"Hamstring problems can be very persistent; you may think you have it licked, and it comes back," says Lisa Alamar, certified structural therapist who has worked with many professional athletes in her Oak Park, Illinois office. "Recurring hamstring problems usually stem from a muscle or structural imbalance between the hamstrings and muscles in the thigh and buttock region."

Recovery

With a mild case, a day off with gentle stretching and massage should make the pain go away. If it persists, use ice and aspirin or ibuprofen and elevate the legs to help bring down the inflammation. An elastic wrap will help reduce the pull on the inflamed area. Some sports medicine physicians may recommend heat after a few days to improve circulation in the area.

Training Adjustments

Depending on the severity of the tear, some light running may be approved by your sports physician 48 hours after the injury. If you continue to run, be sure to go easy on the hamstrings by taking short strides and avoiding downhill running or banked tracks. Water running is an excellent alternative exercise to reduce the strain on the hamstrings.

Prevention

Though hamstrings will always be weaker than quadriceps, most sports physicians recommend hamstring curls and other strength-training exercises that will give you better muscle balance. (Hamstrings should be at least 60 to 70 percent as strong as the quadriceps). Frequent stretching of the hamstrings is also recommended.

Iliotibial Band Syndrome

The iliotibial band is located on the outer side of the leg, from the hip to the knee. Common to both runners and cyclists, iliotibial band syndrome is an inflammation caused by the iliotibial band tendons rubbing against the outer bone of the knee. The pain is usually located on the outside portion of the knee, but irritation may occur anywhere between the knee and the buttocks. Though the pain is not disabling, unless corrected, this injury can persistently ruin your workouts.

"Iliotibial band syndrome is a relatively minor injury that should be treated by solving any mechanical problems, calming the muscle, increasing flexibility, and improving strength," says Robert P. Nirschl, MD, orthopedic surgeon, and Medical Director of the Virginia Sports Medicine Institute. In cases where the injury is relatively minor, massage may also prove to be an effective treatment.

Recovery

If your injury is due to a structural imbalance, orthotics may be all you need. (These are shoe insoles that replace the generic ones that come with shoes. The best orthotics are custom-built by a sports podiatrist to support your unique feet.) If iliotibial band syndrome is caused by overuse, you simply need to decrease the intensity for a week or two. Icing the area and taking aspirin or ibuprofen may help bring down the inflammation.

Training Adjustments

Try water running or light cycling. Avoid high-intensity workouts until the injury is healed. This includes hills or any type of varying terrain that can cause the injury to reoccur.

Prevention Tips

Implement a regular stretching and strengthening program, with particular emphasis on the outer thigh and knee muscles. Also, don't run on worn-out shoes; the wear on the outside of the heel may cause this nagging malady.

Achilles Tendinitis

Located at the back of the ankle at the junction where the large calf muscles attach to the heel bone, the Achilles tendon is vulnerable to microscopic tears and inflammation from the repetitive motion of running. Achilles tendinitis may be caused by overpronation or by the shortening of the calves brought on by excessive hill running or overtraining. The pain is localized with general tightness in the ankle area. Another sure sign is intense pain when walking on the balls of your foot or your toes.

"It's very common for a runner never to give an injured Achilles tendon a good chance to get healthy," says Boulder sports physician Dr. Hobson. "And if the injury has progressed, the surrounding tissue becomes inflamed, creating a situation where…the chances of the injury recurring are high."

Recovery

Icing the area will help bring down the inflammation. For support, wrap the ankle with elastic bandage or tape (though your main support should be a good running shoe with a stable heel). Some sports physicians recommend moist (never dry) heat before and after low-intensity exercise to help loosen muscles and bring some blood to the area. Orthotics or an elevated heel will most likely be recommended to control overpronation.

Training Adjustments

The Achilles tendon is yet another area of the body that is slow to heal due to poor blood supply. If your sports physician considers it a minor case and if it is caught early enough, he or she may allow low-intensity, light running.

Prevention Tips

Use a good pair of running shoes with a stable heel, and watch for wear along the outer edges of the heel. Avoid steep hill climbing and running on hard surfaces. Stretch the Achilles tendon, calf, and hamstring muscles before and after you run. The best prevention is strength training for all the lower leg muscles, a vulnerable part of the body that is subject to high stress from running.

Plantar Fasciitis (Heel Pain)

The plantar fascia is a ligament that runs through the arch of the foot. During the impact of running, the ligament is stretched each time the body's weight is distributed throughout the foot. Plantar fasciitis is caused by overtraining, foot imbalances, or running on hard surfaces or in worn-out shoes. All these things may cause overstretching and strain of the ligament, resulting in tiny tears that lead to inflammation. The pain and area of tenderness is located underneath the foot, at the front of the heel. Usually, the onset of pain is gradual, but increases with continued running. A common symptom of plantar fasciitis is intense pain when awakening in the morning, especially with the first few steps.

Recovery

Plantar fasciitis is considered a serious running injury; if it's not treated properly, further tearing could cause severe damage and take several months to heal. Consult a sports podiatrist for expert treatment. (He will most likely recommend the use of orthotics.) Self-therapy should include ice and aspirin or ibuprofen to relieve inflammation.

Training Adjustments

In severe cases, though it may be a tough prescription to swallow, any activity that puts pressure on your foot is not recommended. (Swimming, preferably with a pull buoy, is a good alternative.) In very mild cases, most sports physicians will allow light running.

Prevention tips

Most running coaches recommend the use of orthotics, even if you don't have any foot problems. Also stretch the plantar fascia. Avoid running on hard surfaces, and don't run on worn-out shoes that have little or no cushioning.

Chapter 10

Peaking to Race

> "Sometimes when I consider what tremendous conse-
> quences come from little things, I am tempted to think
> there are no little things."
>
> —*Bruce Barton*

George Sheehan said that "The race, where I can be a hero, is a contest where I give my word of honor to go out and do battle with myself." He's right. The race is today's equivalent of a battlefield. But instead of fighting an opponent, we are doing battle with ourselves with every stroke, pedaling motion, and stride. Whether they be triathlons, running races, or cycling time trials, races are personal arenas for heroism. Whatever race goal you have set for yourself, you owe it to yourself to have a good race. The key to having a good race is proper training first and then making sure you cover all those little details.

Details, Details

Don't fall into the pre-event bloopers that these guys do:

- The careless triathlete who trains for six months or more to compete in a sprint distance triathlon, only to experience stomach pains during a race from eating a super burrito supreme just minutes before the start.
- The mechanically challenged (you know who you are out there) who don't bother to check the air pressure in their tires, only to find themselves riding on their rims through the transition area.
- Those type A's who can't resist the temptation of putting in one last hard run the day before the big race, only to find that they just don't have fresh legs when they get on the bike (duh).

Isn't it ironic that some people train so long and hard, only to sabotage their efforts by paying little or no attention to some small (but definitely not minor) details that can dramatically affect the outcome of a race? The last thing you want to do after putting in all that work is to blow it by botching a little thing like the wrong meal before a race, failing to tend to a mechanical problem, or a poorly timed hard workout. In the weeks before an event, it's the little things, the small details, that count.

The finish line should be an exhilarating experience, whether you're first or last.

Sweating the details doesn't just help you avoid disaster. It can help you be more mentally and physically prepared to have a great day out there. By making sure all the details we'll focus on in this chapter are covered, you'll feel more confident, better prepared, and ready to peak for the big event.

What to Do in the Weeks Before a Race

First things first, congratulate yourself. You are a few weeks away from what may be one of the most rewarding efforts you'll make in your life. You've made it this far, and you're still standing (hopefully). Training for a triathlon, even for a sprint distance, is no small task. It takes commitment, self-discipline, and an unfaltering capacity for bearing with aches and pains.

You've made it through the scorching hot and humid summer runs when garden sprinklers were few and far between. You've weathered the chilly spring mornings on your bike, when you wished your helmet had a heater. You've tolerated inconsiderate toddlers invading your lap swimming lane. You've come a long way and are probably in better shape than 99 percent of the population. Take pride in your accomplishment. You're ready to complete your first triathlon, up the distance, or go for a personal best. Whatever your goal, congratulate yourself on just getting to where you are now.

But don't pat yourself on the back for too long. You've still got a few weeks to go. Even if your training hasn't been perfect or you've overtrained a little, the next few weeks are the critical zone, a period where it's absolutely essential that you pay attention to some vital details.

Complete Your Last Long Run

Running takes the greatest toll on your body, so make sure you give yourself plenty of time to recover before your race. You should do your last long run, but not your longest, approximately 14 days before the race. Run a distance roughly equivalent to half of your longest previous run. Some triathletes run their longest run on this day, but elite runners have ideal muscle composition for running (predominantly slow-twitch fibers) that allow for quick recovery. The majority of triathletes require more time, so your longest run should be three to four weeks before race day.

Stick to the Tapering Schedule You've Set for Yourself

If you've been following the training advice in part II, tapering will already be built into your training calendar. Too often, triathletes find this phase of training the most mentally difficult to deal with. The thinking usually goes something like this, "I've been training hard.

My body has adapted well. I'm in great shape for the big race. Why in the world would I want to let up?"

Believe it or not, if you've trained as hard as you think you have, your body has to recover from the cumulative mileage you've put on your feet, legs, and arms. Although you may feel just fine, there are likely microscopic tears in your muscle tissue, tears that need a few weeks of easy training and a few rest days to completely heal.

If you have any doubts about the value of tapering and are itching to just blow your training plan to hell, consider a little scientific evidence. A recent study at Malaspina College in British Columbia and the University of Alberta shows exactly how necessary tapering is to triathletes. In the study, 25 athletes trained for an hour five days a week for six weeks at a high-intensity level of 75 to 85 percent. After six weeks, seven athletes tapered for three days, cutting down on volume (not intensity), and a second group tapered for six days. A third group tapered by doing no exercise at all for four full days, and an unfortunate bunch in the fourth group exercised at the same intensity and volume until test day (equivalent to race day).

The results showed a 12-percent increase of the lactate acid threshold level in both the three-day and six-day taper groups. (For the purposes of this study, the lactate acid threshold was a measure of how long a certain exercise intensity could be maintained.) The "no-exercise" group made no improvement, and the "train-to-death" group *decreased* their lactate threshold level.

Glycogen levels were also measured. (Remember, your glycogen storage is like a fuel tank; the more glycogen you have, the longer you can go.) Glycogen storage levels soared by 25 percent with the six-day program. The three-day and the "no exercise" groups showed an increase of 12 percent. Once again, the "train to death" group smelled of overtraining: their glycogen levels *dropped* 12 percent.

"My focus was the cellular level, finding the physiological results of tapering. Of course, everybody wants to know about performance," says J.P. Neary, PhD, who headed the study. "The results determine that a little extra rest helps cells work more efficiently during exercise."

Neary emphasizes that tapering is subject to a host of variables specific to the individual and the training event. For example, a half-Ironman distance race requires longer, slower training than used in the study, and older athletes tend to require longer recovery times. Thus triathletes training for longer distances may do better with more tapering; older triathletes may also need more tapering. The point of all of this is to stick to the tapering suggestions and sample tapering charts presented in chapter 7. Don't let the excitement of the pending drama or your impatience ruin your chances of having a great race.

Watch Your Diet

There are a few important areas to consider concerning your diet in the weeks preceding the big event:

- If you've been following the recommended 65 to 70 percent carbohydrate diet for a triathlete, your pantry should be well-stocked with pasta, grains, fruits, and vegetables. (If not, do some shopping.)
- Are you staying away from high-fat foods like cheese, whole milk, and butter? Make an effort to fine-tune your diet. If you haven't been a good boy or girl, make a commitment to get your nutritional act together in the coming critical weeks. You've come too far to let diet stop you from being your very best. The key word here is fine-tune. Don't make any last-minute drastic diet changes that will be hard on your body.
- If you have a deficiency of protein in your diet, integrate some legumes, egg whites, and low-fat dairy products into your diet.
- Are you keeping well hydrated? Make sure you drink 6 to 10 eight-ounce glasses of water a day.

Try Some Mental Training

You've come far in your physical training, but have you trained your mind with positive thoughts and visualization of the finish line? If not, devote some time to this important, but often overlooked, detail.

Begin to set aside 15 to 30 minutes every day in a quiet place where you won't be interrupted. Close your eyes and relax. Take deep, slow breaths, inhaling through your month and exhaling through your nose. Visualize every phase of the race, from starting line to the glorious finish. See yourself relaxed and confident on the day of the race. You're calm and cool within the hustle and bustle of the crowd. See as much detail as possible, and feel an eager anticipation to meet the challenge that awaits you. If you're not used to meditating, visualizing may seem difficult at first. Persist, as you've done with your physical training.

Test Your Pre-Race Meal

The weeks before a race are a good time to experiment with your ideal pre-race meal. Try eating a high-carbohydrate snack, such as a bagel and banana, 60 to 90 minutes before a moderate to long workout to ensure you don't experience nausea. Another good pre-race meal is an energy bar containing about 40 to 50 carbohydrates with eight ounces of water at least 60 to 90 minutes prior to the race. If you do experience nausea, your stomach may be sensitive. Try something else, or try timing your pre-race meal so that you eat it as long as two hours before you start exercising.

Some sports products are specifically designed to be easily digestible, such as several of the products we covered in chapter 8. You may want to test out some of these as pre-event meals during your training:

- A carbo-loading and recovery drink
- A balanced nutrition shake with plenty of carbohydrates, moderate protein, and low fat content
- Carbohydrate gels and energy bars

Practice Your Transitions

Now is a good time to practice your swim-to-bike transition, known as "T1" in tri-speak, and your bike-to-run transition, known as, you guessed it, "T2" (named after Terminator 2, a great multisport motivational flick—Linda Hamilton's training regimen will get you psyched).

Practice your T1 transitions on a beach. Set up a mock transition area at an open water swim site and have somebody watch your stuff while you swim. Lay everything you're going to need on a towel, just like you will do at the race transition area (I'll give you a checklist later in this chapter). Don't make this a long workout. Swim a short distance, practice getting out of your wetsuit (if you'll be wearing one), change into your bike gear, and go for a short ride.

Practice your T2 transition on another day. Again, set up a mock transition area, but this time you can set it up on your doorstep. Go for a short bike ride, and then change into your running gear and go for a short run. Although you should have already done some brick workouts, these practices should focus on making smooth transitions and getting used to the gear and clothing (if any) changes. You should also decide how you want to approach the transitions.

Essentially, there are two ways of transitioning: the fast way and the comfortable way.

The Fast Way

The fast way means essentially racing in your swimsuit. The benefit is obvious: a quick transition. The drawbacks are also obvious: saddle soreness and, if it's a cool day, goosebumps. Most triathletes competing in sprint or Olympic distance triathlons choose to go this route. Riding in a swimsuit is tolerable for most people for these relatively short distances, and if you've wisely purchased a triathlon swimsuit with some padding, that will help as well.

The Comfortable Way

If you have personal reasons for not riding and running in your swimsuit or feel that bike shorts will make a big difference in terms

Getting that darned wetsuit off can be the most challenging part of your first transition.

of comfort, then by all means, take your time and slip them on over your swimsuit. (Most triathlons of shorter distances don't have changing areas, and being naked in the transition area is cause for disqualification and possible arrest!) Feel free to stop and don cycling shorts, cycling jersey, and any other clothing that you feel will help you maintain comfort. Of course, all that extra dressing will add to your transition time. But if you're just doing the triathlon to finish, who cares?

Whether you run with or without socks depends on how sensitive your feet are. Again, most triathletes forgo this for shorter distances, but that doesn't mean you have to. An inexpensive and helpful item to make your running shoe transition quick are lace locks. These neat little gadgets attach to your shoelaces and make tying your shoes as simple as tightening the laces and pulling down. They are surprisingly solid and dependable, tightening your laces as well as a double knot.

Unless you feel an insatiable need to show off your new duds, there's really no need for running shorts. One exception may be if you're wearing bulky cycling shorts, which may chafe your groin area and be a nuisance on the run. If that's the case, go ahead and put on those running shorts over your swimsuit.

Finalize Travel Arrangements

Will you be traveling to your race? If so, are there any special travel arrangements you need to make, such as confirming hotel reservations? Make arrangements well in advance so that you're not worrying about these details the day before a race.

Don't Make Any Equipment Changes

Now is *not* the time to make any equipment changes, such as a new bike or a different saddle position. If you've been training with no problems with your current equipment and bike position, then there's no reason to change. Changing these factors in the weeks before a race could hurt you or, worse, cause injury. Even swimming goggles can take a few workouts to fit your face properly, so stick with what you've got now unless you absolutely have to change because of breakage, theft, or any other factor that necessitates replacement.

You may be able to get away with purchasing new running shoes two weeks before an event, but one week would be stretching it.

Melanie's Race Advice: Knowledge and Preparation the Key

Melanie Mocium's first race was promising, until she reached the transition area. She exited the water at the 1994 Donner Lake Triathlon in front of the top women in her age group. When it came time to hop on the bike, she quickly lost her lead because of her lack of knowledge and preparation. Although the race was Olympic distance, she changed into cycling and running gear during the transitions under a large beach towel. Although many triathletes opt to do this for longer distances, in hindsight, Melanie wishes she had talked to other triathletes and learned about faster transitioning options before her first race.

"I just did everything wrong for what I wanted to accomplish," says the 44-year-old triathlete from Mill Valley, California. "I finished 10th in my age group, which was great, but I could have done a lot better if I was prepared."

In another race, Melanie was led off the run leg of a half-Ironman course on the ninth mile by a volunteer and ran nearly two miles extra. Although the majority of race volunteers can be depended upon to point you in the right direction, mistakes do happen. As Melanie points out, this incident illustrates the value of knowing the course beforehand. "Don't assume anything in a race," says Melanie. "Be familiar with the swim, bike, and run course so you know what to expect."

Today's running shoes don't take as long to break in as older models did because of high-tech materials and design. Still, it's best to be on the safe side unless you absolutely need to replace them.

Many triathlons hold expos the day before the event takes place, and often you can get some great deals on bicycle stuff and multisport products. Many novice triathletes get carried away and purchase new equipment they intend to use the next day. Don't do it! Sure, go ahead and snag some great steals, but save it for the next event. Put simply, you should always train with new equipment before you try it during a race.

What to Do Days Before the Race

The few days preceding your first triathlon may be a little nerve-racking. For the water-challenged, feelings of impending doom may haunt you, and butterflies may occasionally flutter around in your stomach. Even if you've done a few multisport events, any new, challenging, or longer distance race may have a similar effect.

These feelings are completely normal, and you should take every opportunity to find comfort in the pages of your triathlon logbook (you've been keeping one, haven't you?). You've done the homework, and even though you may be nervous, you'll do just fine. Talk to training partners and other triathletes who have been through it. Log onto any triathlon chat room on the Internet (see "For More Information . . .") and seek reassurance. If you've trained properly, any triathlete will tell you that you'll have a wonderful experience.

Beside taking care of your mental state, here are a few other reminders and suggestions for the days before a race:

• **Do a safety check on your bike.** The one piece of equipment most likely to break down is your bike, so you'd be smart to do a safety check. Look for any parts that may have loosened as a result of the countless miles of training you've put in. Tighten your stem, aero bars, seatpost, pedals—anything that might be loose. Check your brakes, and look for any cuts or slits in your tires. If you're not mechanically inclined, take your bike to a local shop that you trust, but make sure they can do a quick safety check of your bike while you wait. You don't want to be stuck the night before a race with your bike in the shop.

• **Eat right.** Pay special attention to your diet in the days preceding your race. Stay away from high-fat foods and try not to eat too late. Eat healthy snacks. Focus on eating high-carbohydrate meals. Drink plenty of liquids.

• **Pick up your race packet.** Some races require you or give you the option of picking up your race number, T-shirt, and goodie bag the day before the race. If not, you'll have to sort through that stuff on race morning.

• **Attend pre-race meetings.** Many major races hold a pre-race meeting the day before the event. Even if attendance is not required, it's a good idea for novice triathletes to attend. These meetings

To Load or Not to Load?

You've probably heard of carbo-loading, which was described briefly in chapter 8. The idea behind carbohydrate-loading is simple. As we discussed, carbohydrates are the best source of glycogen, a clean-burning fuel ideally suited for high-energy efforts. The problem is that, like a gas tank in a car, our muscles can only hold so much glycogen before they run dry.

When that happens, look out. Usually some time after 20 miles in a marathon, you may "hit the wall," or more specifically, feel like a Mack truck flattened you. You may experience loss of energy and overwhelming fatigue, nausea—any number of different, unpleasant symptoms depending on your body's unique physiology. Although this physiological phenomenon is somewhat different in bicycling, cyclists often refer to this experience as bonking. It feels just like it sounds folks. Your tongue might be hanging over your handlebar, and if you haven't gotten enough liquids, the inside of your mouth might feel fur-lined.

The purpose of carbo-loading is to offset (and possibly avoid) such occurrences in events lasting over two hours. In effect, you are trying to create a bigger gas tank, a greater reserve of glycogen to delay running on fumes. Notice that I said events lasting over two hours. If you're getting ready to complete a sprint distance triathlon, you don't need to even consider carbo-loading. Even for an Olympic distance race, the benefits of carbo-loading are negligible.

If you're training regularly and eating a diet composed mainly of carbohydrates, just keep doing what you're doing because you're already carbohydrate-loading to some degree. (That was easy, huh?) The process of pushing your body harder and harder every day, with proper rest and recovery and in conjunction with a high-carbohydrate diet, increases the capacity of your muscles to hold glycogen reserves. Taking advantage of the carbohydrate window and ingesting carbo-hydrates immediately after exercise (as discussed in chapter 8) also helps the body to hold more glycogen reserves in the future.

typically cover topics such as water temperature, course descriptions, rules, grounds for disqualification, and other important information.

• **Make sure you know the wheres and whens.** Do you know the directions to the race site? Do you know where to park? What time does your age group wave start? All of this information should be covered in your race packet, if you get it the day before. If not, make sure you contact the race office and get this information a few days before. Don't wait until the night before; more often than not, the race office staff is out setting up the course or too busy to handle your call.

• **Prepare everything the night before.** Give yourself a few hours the night before a race to get all your gear together. Don't wait until after midnight to be scrambling around, putting your stuff together. If you've picked up your race packet, pin your number to a piece of clothing you'll be wearing, and tie in any number cards or place stickers the race folks may have given you to put on your bike or helmet. Many triathletes who race in their swimsuit use a race belt, an elastic belt that you can pin your number to that quickly snaps around your waist. If you'll be using one, pin your race number to it.

Set out the clothing you'll be wearing tomorrow morning. This should include your swimsuit, which will go on underneath whatever you'll be wearing as you head out to the race. Pack a gym bag of everything you'll need for the race. Use the checklist on page 192 to make sure you don't forget anything.

Get a Good Night's Sleep

Make sure you request a wake-up call or set your alarm so that you have plenty of time to get ready for the big race day. You don't want to be rushing, which will only add to the nervousness you may feel on race morning. Do whatever relaxes you before you go to bed: listen to music, soak in the tub, have a hot cup of tea. Try to get to bed early. It may take awhile before the jitters wear off and you fall asleep. If, despite all your efforts, you get to bed late or the jitters keep you up, don't worry about your lack of sleep. It won't affect you during the race. Sleep deprivation is only a factor when it's cumulative, say over a period of days or even weeks.

What to Do on Race Morning

Unless you're the bravest man or woman in the world, you'll probably be pretty nervous. Just try to relax and focus on getting everything in your car that you need for the race. If time permits, try to do something relaxing—listen to music, or ask your spouse nicely (please honey) to massage your shoulders and scalp.

• **Time your pre-race meal right.** Almost all of us has had the experience of having some sort of stomach distress, whether it be

Race Bag Checklist

I've found the best way to make sure I've packed everything I need for racing is to break down triathlon gear by category, which I've narrowed down to four:

Swim Gear

Swimsuit (place this with the clothes you'll be wearing race morning)

Goggles

Antifog drops for goggles (optional)

Wetsuit (optional)

Swim cap (the race has probably provided one for you)

Bike Gear

Helmet (make sure you attach any race number stickers that may have been provided)

Bike shoes (optional)

Socks (optional for shorter races)

Cycling shorts (optional for shorter races)

Cycling jersey (optional for shorter races)

Cycling glasses (optional, but recommended)

Water bottles (filled with water or a fluid-replacement drink)

Spare tubes

Tools

Running Gear

Running shoes

Race number (attached to a race belt or your running shorts, T-shirt, or singlet)

Socks (optional)

Running shorts (optional for shorter races)

Running T-shirt or singlet (optional for shorter races)

Headband, visor, or cap (optional)

Sunglasses (optional)

> ### *Race Support Gear*
>
> Sport watch
>
> Fluid-replacement drink, energy bars, or snacks
>
> Jacket (in case of rain or cool weather)
>
> Sport sunscreen
>
> Water-based lubricant (to rub in areas where wetsuit chafing may occur or during running and cycling)
>
> Towel (to set out everything you need during the race and provide a place to sit during your transitions)

nausea, side stitches, or diarrhea, during exercise. Although during a race these conditions can be attributed to nervousness, many times they are caused by eating a pre-race meal too close to the starting time of an event. As indicated in chapter 8, it's important to eat your pre-race meal well before the race, at least an hour before the start or, for sensitive stomachs or bigger meals, as long as two hours prior to the start.

• **Get to the transition area one hour before the start.** First-timers may even want to get there 90 minutes or two hours before the start, especially if it's a city event with huge participation numbers. Getting there early gives you plenty of time to park and walk to the transition area (in big events, you may be parked as much as a mile from the race site).

• **Park your bike and get your body marked.** When you walk your bike and carry your gym bag to the transition area, you'll most likely be greeted by security personnel who will ask to see your race number. Park your bike on the bike racks provided; hang your bicycle handlebars over the railing. In many races, bike rack positions are preassigned according to your race number, so look for your number and park your bike there. Before you start unpacking your gym bag, seek out body markers, race volunteers who will write your race number on your arms and legs. These numbers help identify you when you're coming out of the swim and onto the bike.

Make sure you get to a race with plenty of time to organize your transition area. Always have the rest of your gear nearby, in case you need something you haven't set out.

- **Set up your personal transition station.** Lay out your towel next to your bike. Don't be a hog about space—just use enough room to set out your gear. Place the cycling and running gear you'll be using during the race in logical progression, with the cycling stuff on the half of the towel closest to you. Make sure everything is easily accessible. The photo above is a good example of an organized transition area.
- **Get ready to swim.** If you're wearing a wetsuit, slip it on. Make sure to dab some water-based lubricant in areas that might chafe, such as armpits and the groin. No need to zip up the top half if the race won't start for a while and it's a hot day. Check your goggle straps and have your swim cap ready.
- **Check out the lay of the land.** Once you've got your gear organized and you're ready to swim, take a walk around the transition area.

    1. Notice where your bike is racked. Are there any distinguishable markers or landmarks that will help you find your bike

Transition Setup Tips

Here are some tips to make your TI and T2 go more smoothly.

- Have a water bottle handy for a quick sip after the swim.
- If you're going to wear cycling shoes, undo the Velcro™ straps or laces so that you won't have to fumble around with them.
- Make sure all the water bottles on the bike are filled.
- Put your bike in an easy gear for a quick start.
- Place your cycling glasses inside your helmet so that you don't forget to put them on.
- If you've opted for socks on the bike and/or run, put them in your cycling or running shoes.
- Loosen your running shoelaces for quick entry.
- Place the race belt (or whatever article of clothing you've attached your race number to) next to sunglasses, cap, or anything else you'll be wearing on the run.

quickly after the swim? Some triathletes bring balloons or colorful flags to help with this issue, but all you really need is some permanent landmark near your bike. Another option is to count the number of bike rack rows to your bike from the swim-to-bike transition area entrance.

2. Find out where you'll be exiting the transition area on your bike and where you'll be exiting on the run. Make a mental note of these directions. Volunteers are sometimes positioned in the transition area to point the way to groggy, disoriented, or tired triathletes, but don't depend on help.

3. Take a walk to the beach and see whether you can get a feel for the swim course from shore. You should have some knowledge of the shape of the swim course from the race information provided to you, but it helps to have a look for yourself. Will the swim buoys always be on your right or left? How many turns are there? If it's a hazy day and you can't tell from the shore, ask any race officials who may be present.

- **Take a quick pre-race dip.** No need to do any long swimming, but it helps to dive into the water a few minutes before the start. Most

There are some races that start in deep water, so brush up on your water-treading skills.

races allow for a warm-up area, as long as you get out of the way when the race begins. Taking a quick dip helps offset some of the initial shock of the water, especially if temps are a bit on the chilly side. A pre-race dip is especially helpful for those wearing wetsuits. A thin layer of water will seep into the wetsuit (which is normal) and create a warming barrier for you, if given enough time to be heated by your body.

• **Seed yourself properly in your swim wave.** Very few races have mass starts nowadays, so you'll most likely be swimming with peers of your own age group. If you are a novice swimmer, have any reservations about open water swimming, or are competing in your first triathlon, position yourself at the back of the pack or off to the side. This way, you'll hopefully avoid any unnecessary body contact.

What to Do (and Not Do) During a Race

As with anything in life, a myriad of things can go wrong during a race: a kick in the head during the swim, a flat tire during the bike ride, a blister on your foot during the run. Solid preparation beforehand will often help minimize any unexpected surprises. Another key to having a good race is intelligently handling the variables you can control.

Keep Your Head During the Swim

Even if you do seed yourself properly, body contact may still occur during the swim. It may be as mildly unsettling as grazing another swimmer's arm with yours or as startling as a kick in the face. Keep your wits about you and be aware of other swimmers in your immediate area. If you do have the misfortune of playing open water swimming's version of bumper cars, keep calm and simply make adjustments. If you have to, stop and tread water, letting other swimmers too close to you go by (only be careful that nobody behind swims into you). If you are a particularly slow swimmer (like me), be prepared for the fast fish in the waves behind you to come zooming by you like speedboats. Again, be aware of them, keep calm, and let them pass you by without incident.

Prepare for Smooth Transitions

Triathlon is a paradox. You need to be in the present moment to race your best, but you also need to mentally and physically prepare for what comes next. (Is that philosophical, or what?) Transitions give you that window of opportunity to jump to the next activity, but even transitions require a little forethought.

T1 Tips

The swim-to-bike transition is usually characterized by a feeling of disorientation and a general lack of coordination. That's especially true if you're new to open water or just had a rough swim. These tips may help you make a smooth T1:

- It helps if, in the few yards before you come to shore, you mentally envision a smooth transition.
- Be prepared for possible dizziness when you stand up.
- Ease up your pace in the last few yards so that you don't jump out of the water breathless.
- If volunteers are there to help, let them hold you up until you've got your coordination back.
- Unzip your wetsuit as you walk or run to your bike.

Start thinking about what you need to do to prepare for the cycling leg as soon as you finish the swim.

- Look for your landmark or count the number of rows to your bike.
- Drink some fluids.
- Don't forget to strap on your helmet before you get on your bike or else you'll be disqualified.
- Carefully walk or ride your bike out of the transition area, depending on what the race policy is (if you aren't sure, play it safe and walk your bike out of the transition area).

T2 Tips

By far, the T2 transition is the hardest for the first-timer. Although brick workouts should have helped you get accustomed to that tight feeling of coming off the bike and starting to run, nothing quite prepares you for the real thing. Some people have no trouble with T2, but others must deal with cramping and nonexistent runner's legs. These tips may help you make a smooth T2:

- Again, drink plenty of fluids; cramping during the bike-to-run transition may be a symptom of dehydration.
- A mile or so before the end of the bike ride, ease off and pedal in a relatively easy gear.
- Concentrate on smooth pedal strokes and stretching out your leg muscles.

You can save time in a transition by taking your feet out of your bike shoes before getting off the bike.

- Mentally prepare to make the transition to running.
- Be slow and cautious when entering the transition area—most bicycle accidents occur here.
- If your legs are very tight, take the time now to stretch a bit.
- Begin running slowly with short strides, easing into it and increasing your pace as your leg muscles allow.

Stick to the Plan (and the Pace)

It's easy to get so caught up in the hoopla of a race: the huge crowd, the balloons and banners, the noise and music. When the gun (or cannon or horn) goes off, you're so shot up with adrenaline that it's hard to hold yourself back. And if the kids or your significant other is watching, well, you just have to show 'em just how fast daddy or mommy or sweetheart can tear up the triathlon course. Don't do it! You may look impressive during those first few minutes of the swim or from the transition to the bike or run, but you'll soon start to feel the effects before you reach the first buoy or mile marker.

One of the most difficult things for triathletes to learn is pacing. We each have an internal clock, and even during the excitement of a race, we can learn to run by that clock and knock off the miles with consistent and strong splits. The key is to minimize any external influences that can effect your internal clock and sense of pace. Stick to your plan. If you're just racing to finish, don't send your body into oxygen deprivation by sprinting. If performance is on your mind, stay true to the pace that will get you there in the time you want, but also be flexible in case your arms or legs just don't have it.

Drink Plenty of Fluids

We discussed heat illnesses and how to avoid them in chapters 6 and 8, but it's worth noting that it's necessary to drink fluids during a race as well. Even veteran triathletes get so carried away during the heat of the moment that they neglect drinking fluids and end up befriending an IV bottle in the medical tent. The biggest key to avoiding dehydration and heat illness is to stay properly hydrated. Drink fluids immediately after the swim and drink eight ounces of water or a fluid-replacement drink every 15 minutes while you ride. During the run, take advantage of every water station.

Don't be a Dumbo—always make sure you're prepared for the swim start.

Do you need to eat during a race? For sprint distance races, probably not. For Olympic distance races or longer, eating a carbohydrate gel or solid snacks is a good idea (of course, these foods should have already been tested for digestibility during training).

Have Fun

The best advice is to just have some fun out there. Don't take it too seriously and kill yourself. Be courteous and kind to your race colleagues, volunteers, police officers, and spectators. If you intend to make triathlon a healthy and fun lifestyle choice instead of a one-shot, grueling event, keep a big smile on your face as you race. It'll be even bigger when you finish.

Chapter 11

Tri, Tri Again

> "What we do during our working hours determines what we have; what we do in our leisure hours determines who we are."
>
> *—George Eastman*

Like any sport or organization, triathlon has several unspoken and undocumented rules. These codes of ethics are not spelled out in the USA Triathlon handbook, but they are just as applicable to triathletes.

Among the running and triathlon community, for example, there's the race T-shirt rule. The rule is that you should never wear a race T-shirt unless you've finished that race. Dropped out? Got sick? Lightning hit you on the way to the finish line? Then give the shirt to your neighbor. Use it to clean your bike chain. Burn it. But the unspoken rule is that you can't wear the shirt if you haven't done the race.

Among my circle of multisport friends, we have the "license to call yourself a triathlete" rule. Essentially the rule stipulates that you must complete at least one triathlon a year to continue to refer to yourself as a triathlete. No matter how much running, cycling, or swimming you've done during training, you've got to prove your mettle on a race course at least once every 365 days. The one notable exception to this rule is the "lifetime Ironman license" amendment. Should you successfully finish an Ironman distance event, you are hereby awarded a lifetime license to call yourself a triathlete, even if you never do another race.

Yet none of my friends who have completed Ironman distance races have stopped competing or taken a hiatus from training (including myself). Although I planned to take a year-long respite from multisport training after my Ironman finish, I just couldn't do it. The running shoes beckoned. Roads ripe for cycling called for more adventures. The sweet sensation of cool open waters lured me.

During a particularly satisfying run on a pristine trail recently, I realized why I couldn't take time away from multisport training. *This is who I am.* At some point in my 10 years of swimming, biking, and running, triathlon had become an integral part of me as a person. I could no sooner walk away from it for a year than I could stop writing.

Being a Triathlon Lifer

Chances are, you've chosen to participate in multisport events because they challenge you in a way no other activity can. Unlike the common one-time marathon goal, triathletes usually come back for more, and more, and more.

Besides the fun and variety that triathlon training and racing provide, I believe triathletes are usually lifers because of the inevitable positive effects swimming, biking, and running have on the rest of our lives. Although triathlon is certainly not the definitive answer

Triathlon is the kind of positive and gratifying sport that will put a smile on your face, so why not keep it for life?

to everyone's problems, here are some of the changes and influences you may find happening in your life as a result of triathlon:

• **Shedding bad habits.** Hey, we all have them. Those things we do to ourselves that aren't really good for us, but have turned into habits from years of reinforcement. Embracing multisports can be the impetus for unloading some of that annoying baggage. It may be something as dramatic as quitting smoking or something more subtle like overeating, partying all night, or just being too sedentary. You may find yourself not watching as much television and getting outdoors more.

• **Better eating habits.** Something about being fit naturally translates into taking a good look at the foods we eat. Meals are no longer just an opportunity to fill your face; they are a chance to refuel from a hard day's workout. Naturally, you want the best fuel you can get so that tomorrow's workout goes just a little bit better. If excessive body weight is an issue for you, you'll find that triathlon is a great way to help you burn calories.

• **Healthier sleeping patterns.** You may find that you sleep better at night, with less interruption of sleep (providing that you don't work out just before you go to bed and don't overtrain). A good day's training may also require that you get a little more sleep, which can only be beneficial to you.

• **More friends.** Triathlon is a great social sport. No doubt, you'll meet people with similar goals and philosophies and start some lifelong friendships. If you take my advice and go to swim camp and do group rides and runs, you'll have plenty of opportunity to meet like-minded people.

• **Less sickness, more energy.** Studies have shown that regular, moderate exercise (not excessive as in overtraining) can help boost your immune system. You may also find that you have more energy during the day, and working out can help recharge you when your batteries are low.

• **Greater self-discipline.** Training regularly and consistently requires you to keep the promises you make to yourself (via your training schedule). This kind of constant reinforcement instills confidence that you can do what you need to do, regardless of how you are feeling. Focusing on a goal and doing the work that it takes to make that goal a reality will do wonders for your self-esteem and your self-discipline.

Turning Things Around

The moment of truth came for Wes Freas well before crossing his first triathlon finish line. After returning from a family vacation in May of '96, the former competitive college basketball player couldn't believe his eyes. He sat, virtually shell-shocked, at his kitchen table looking at vacation photos. "I saw pictures of me without my shirt on," says the 31-year-old resident of Peoria, Arizona. "I was horrified at what I saw, how much weight I'd gained, and how unhealthy I looked."

Over 70 pounds overweight, he remembered watching the Ironman Triathlon in Hawaii and was introduced to the sport by a friend. He set out to complete his first triathlon the following year, and gradually begun to change his lifestyle. Wes began to eat better, forgoing junk and fast food for complex carbohydrates. The weight came back down, although he had several more bad habits to slay.

"After I did my first few triathlons, I started to feel like a hypocrite," says Wes. "I would look around and see all these fit and healthy people finishing in front of me, and here I was still drinking and chewing tobacco and partying all night. I decided to make some more changes, not because I wanted to be competitive with others, but to compete for myself."

The "copious amounts of beer" and late-night partying ceased. More significantly, he gave up his unhealthiest of habits—six cans of Copenhagen chewing tobacco a day. Now, with a fit and trim body, a healthier outlook on life, and a family that supports him and has joined him on the fitness bandwagon, Wes's next goal is to finish in the top third of his age group. "Three years ago, I didn't have a clue," says Wes. "Now I know how unhealthy my life was, and I never want to go back."

Using Your First Triathlon as a Stepping Stone

The first thing you may ask yourself after crossing the finish line of your first triathlon is, *"What now?"* Once the elation has subsided, it's only natural to feel somewhat hesitant about what this all means and what to do next. To help cure those post-finish line blues and move on to the next step, the following sections suggest ways to help turn the end of your first triathlon into a new beginning.

Get Involved in the Sport

There are countless ways to participate in the sport:

• **Subscribe to a triathlon magazine.** Whether you choose *Inside Triathlon, Triathlete,* or some of the myriad of regional multisports magazines popping up all over the country, subscribing to these periodicals helps you keep abreast of events and trends happening in the sport. You'll also find training columns, equipment reviews, and, if keeping up with pros and top amateurs interests you, race reports. More importantly, you'll find a calendar section and race ads so you can find out all about upcoming races in your area.

• **Join USA Triathlon.** Most triathlons are USA Triathlon-sanctioned, which means you must be a member in order to participate or purchase a one-day membership for a small fee. If you plan on doing several USA Triathlon-sanctioned races in a year, it's worth joining because you'll end up paying more in one-day memberships than the annual fee. You'll also receive a USA Triathlon publication, as well as access to their travel desk and a few other benefits.

• **Join local triathlon clubs.** If you live in or near a major metropolitan area, chances are there's a triathlon club near you. Ask other triathletes or inquire about clubs at local races. Clubs are a great way to socialize and meet training partners.

• **Get on the Net.** The Internet has several triathlon and multisports sites, including bulletin boards and chat rooms where you can post questions or opinions to other triathletes around the world. *Inside Triathlon* also hosts chats with professional triathletes, such as Dave Scott, on a regular basis.

• **Join the political arena.** Many significant issues are facing triathlon, and organizations such as USA Triathlon represent an opportunity for triathletes to have a voice in the future of the sport. Important issues such as drafting and officiating make it imperative that the governing bodies of the sport are represented by grass-roots triathletes willing to give of their time and energy.

• **Volunteer.** Don't wait until you're injured to consider volunteering for a race. Whether you get aid station duty, transition area security, or finish line cleanup, the important thing is that you give back to the sport all the enjoyment and fun you get out of it. Who

Race volunteers are angels sent down from heaven—especially on hot days!

knows, maybe someday you'd like to put on your own triathlon and join the ranks of race directors.

- **Be a coach or mentor.** Whether it's through a club or a youth triathlon training camp, the sport is always in need of good coaches and mentors. For example, at Chicago State University, veteran triathlete Bernard Lyles has created and continues to coordinate a triathlon training program for inner city kids. Through his devotion, and with the help of a team of triathlete volunteers and financial contributions, Lyles continues to change the lives of kids growing up in a very tough environment. Talk to local triathlon clubs for information on similar coaching or mentoring programs. If there isn't one, you could always start your own!

Set Your Sights on Another Goal

The fun doesn't have to end with your first sprint or Olympic distance race. There are plenty of multisport goals you can set your sights on:

Coach, mentor, and Ironman triathlete Bernard Lyles runs a triathlon training program for inner city youths at Chicago State University.

- **Go faster.** When you finish your first triathlon it'll be a personal best no matter what your time is. But perhaps you have this little voice inside you that says you can finish the swim faster, hammer the bike harder, and dash through the run without stopping now that you've got the first-time willies out of your system. Go for it. Try some speedwork, maybe even some interval training. Keep in mind that you'll need to graduate to the next course of triathlon training knowledge to do it safely.

    By reading multisport magazines and books that cover more advanced endurance and triathlon training techniques, you can further your knowledge and broaden your workout arsenal. As you'll no doubt find, you'll be advised to consider integrating strength training into your schedule. Of course, investing in a faster, lighter, more aerodynamic triathlon bicycle may also be on the horizon.

- **Go farther.** More than a decade ago, triathlon journalist Mike Plant pegged the Hawaiian Ironman Triathlon as the "holy grail" of triathletes. The nickname has stuck. To this day, triathletes look upon the shores of Kona as the ultimate proving grounds for their mettle.

You may not now, or ever, have the desire to finish an Ironman distance race, but perhaps someday the half-Ironman may hold some fascination for you.

• **Swim, bike, or run.** You may find that you have a talent in one particular sport and prefer to see how well you can do with it. Tour de France cyclist Lance Armstrong was the sprint distance Triathlon World Champion before he ever became involved in world-class cycling. Perhaps the prospect of completing a bicycle century (100 miles) ride, or running a marathon excites you.

A Glimpse at the Ironman

As a newcomer to the sport, you are probably focused on sprint or Olympic distances, and the Ironman distance may not be on your horizon at all or, at the very least, may be a few years away. But more

Gus: a real iron man.

than likely, you have some curiosity about what it takes to do an Ironman distance event and the experience of finishing such a grueling race. Having just completed the Great Floridian race in Clermont, Florida, an Ironman distance event, I have a few quick training facts and some thoughts about my experience.

My Ironman Training Snapshot

Before I got on the plane to Florida, I printed out my training totals from the workout log on my computer: 150,000 yards of swimming, 3,500 miles of cycling, and 700 miles of running. In all, I had put in close to 400 hours of training (sounds impressive, but it's actually on the light side for Ironman training). Here are some other facts:

- I gave myself a year to train (with 10 years of multisport experience and a dozen half-Ironman distance finishes to my credit).
- My goal was solely to finish, so my running and cycling training consisted almost entirely of long, slow workouts (base training) designed to simply cover long distances.
- I swam a long swim of an hour or more every other week and concentrated on drills and technique during the remainder of my five weekly pool workouts.
- In total, I put in roughly a dozen 100-mile-plus rides, many of which were organized century rides put on by bike clubs.
- My long runs were between 14 and 21 miles, which I would do once a week.
- My biggest challenge was finding the right saddle (it took me three purchases). After about 50 miles, this makes a big difference!

The Ironman Experience

Everyone experiences an Ironman differently. The one universal experience is a sense of great pride and joy in the accomplishment. Having trained just to finish my experience was more relaxed than the more competitive triathletes racing. This no-pressure approach helped me to embrace the struggle, as I took the time to thank race volunteers at the aid stations and spectators along the course.

Time has passed since my first Ironman finish. As with most key life experiences, it's easy to dismiss or forget their importance. Yet I count not just crossing the finish line, but the year-long training and the 15-plus hours it took me to complete the event, as one of the most enjoyable and rewarding times of my life.

Ending Thoughts: It's About Time

Time is a curious thing. As you begin to participate in the sport of triathlon, time may take on a greater significance. You'll no doubt measure the time it takes to swim, T1, bike, T2, and run with much apprehension, sometimes disappointment, most times joy.

I read something the other day about time that struck me as fascinating. The ancient Greeks distinguished time as "chronos time" or "kairos time." Chronos time is clock time, the usual linear way we have at looking at time. As busy human beings living in a harried, hurried society, we are continually focused on chronos time. We carry wallet-sized computers that organize our lives into neat little chunks of time on a three-gigabit hard drive. We set our 2,000-function, 100-split memory sport watches to beep at every stride and to catch every mile marker. We obsess over the three minutes that we're trying to nip off our commute time from work.

Kairos time is what some have called "soul time." It is usually a time of intensity, of pattern interruption, or a change in direction. We don't often realize kairos time when it's happening, usually because we're too busy *experiencing* a life-changing belief or revelation. Others characterize kairos time as a shift in perception, a "paradigm shift" as author Stephen Covey puts it in *The Seven Habits of Highly Effective People.* Put simply, kairos time is those glorious moments in which you have a deeper understanding of the mystery of life and a fleeting peek into your own soul.

When I look back upon my experiences as a triathlete, I realize that I've been fortunate to have had many moments of kairos time—each time I crosssed a triathlon finish line. Usually, everything moves in slow motion. I can feel my heartbeat as though it were a tribal drum. Mostly, I experience a pervading sense of wonder at what can be accomplished with a little perseverance.

Those moments are hard to duplicate. Time, like life, is funny that way. But triathlon is one of the few activities we can indulge in where the likelihood of kairos time is much greater, and the possibility of peeking into our own souls for a few quick, sacred moments is there with every splash, mash, and dash. As you embark upon your new multisport adventure, more than wishing you smooth transitions or fast times, I wish you many, many moments of kairos time.

Blank Training Grids ▬

Here are your blank training grids. You may photocopy them for your convenience. If you prefer 8 1/2 × 11 sheets, copy them at 145%.

My Base Training Schedule

SWIMMING	Mon	
	Tue	
	Wed	
	Thu	
	Fri	
	Sat	
	Sun	
CYCLING	Mon	
	Tue	
	Wed	
	Thu	
	Fri	
	Sat	
	Sun	
RUNNING	Mon	
	Tue	
	Wed	
	Thu	
	Fri	
	Sat	
	Sun	

Tip: circle or highlight your key workouts.

My Speed and Technique Training Schedule

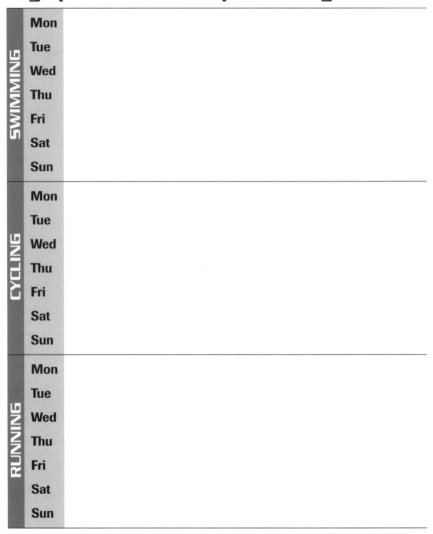

SWIMMING	Mon	
	Tue	
	Wed	
	Thu	
	Fri	
	Sat	
	Sun	
CYCLING	Mon	
	Tue	
	Wed	
	Thu	
	Fri	
	Sat	
	Sun	
RUNNING	Mon	
	Tue	
	Wed	
	Thu	
	Fri	
	Sat	
	Sun	

Tip: don't forget to allow yourself one rest day every week.

My Race Simulation Training Schedule

SWIMMING	Mon	
	Tue	
	Wed	
	Thu	
	Fri	
	Sat	
	Sun	
CYCLING	Mon	
	Tue	
	Wed	
	Thu	
	Fri	
	Sat	
	Sun	
RUNNING	Mon	
	Tue	
	Wed	
	Thu	
	Fri	
	Sat	
	Sun	

Tip: practice your navigational skills in open water.

My Tapering Schedule

SWIMMING		
	Mon	
	Tue	
	Wed	
	Thu	
	Fri	
	Sat	
	Sun	

CYCLING		
	Mon	
	Tue	
	Wed	
	Thu	
	Fri	
	Sat	
	Sun	

RUNNING		
	Mon	
	Tue	
	Wed	
	Thu	
	Fri	
	Sat	
	Sun	

Tip: remember, don't do any hard or long workouts in the days before a race.

Tri-Jargon Glossary

Do you know the difference between an aero bar and a Power Bar®? What about the difference between hammering and spinning? Like any sport, triathlon has its share of jargon. Some of it is unique to multisports, but much of it originates from swimming, cycling, and running. I've tried to explain some of the more popular triathlon terms in this book, but this glossary provides more complete descriptions to help you speak the tri-language.

aero bar. Short for aerodynamic handlebar, a bicycle accessory known to provide a significant time savings advantage on the bike.

body marking. The practice of race volunteers writing your race number on your legs and arms upon your arrival at the transition area before a race. This is done with a big, black magic marker to help keep track of you when you exit the swim or start the bike leg. Don't worry, the markings rub off with a little soap and water, but egotistical triathletes like to wash around these markings to show off their triathlete status in front of their non-triathlete friends (okay, I'll admit it, I've done it).

bonk. Similar to hitting the wall at the latter stages of a marathon, this is a term cyclists use to describe the point during extended endurance exercise when glycogen reserves are depleted, causing overwhelming fatigue, nausea, or any number of different, unpleasant symptoms.

BOPer. Back-of-the-pack triathlete (someone who typically finishes races as volunteers take down the finish line sign).

brain freeze. The sensation experienced when jumping into a very cold open water swim.

bricks. Short for brick workouts, which are either swim-to-bike or bike-to-run training sessions designed to simulate triathlon racing conditions and help the body adapt to transitioning from one sport to the next.

bullethead. Triathlete in a swim cap.

cadence. A number that measures revolutions per minute (RPMs) of the pedaling stroke on the bike.

drafting. In cycling, riding closely behind another rider or group of riders to reduce wind drag by as much as 40 percent. This tactic is used in road racing, but it's not allowed in the triathlon (with the exception of a few races that allow only the professionals to draft). In swimming, following behind another competitor in their slipstream, thus reducing effort by as much as 10 to 20 percent. This is allowed in triathlon and often utilized by competitive triathletes hoping to conserve energy for the bike and run.

fishing. Reeling in all the fast swimmers with weak cycling ability on the bike leg.

gazelle. A talented, fast runner.

greyhound. See *gazelle*.

hammer. Going hard and fast on the bike, as in "Dude, you really hammered that bike course." It can also imply that the rider is pushing big gears.

ice-cream headache. See *brain freeze*.

IM. Abbreviation for Ironman distance. Also used to abbreviate specific Ironman races (for example, IMA is Ironman Australia, IMC is Ironman Canada, and IMH is Ironman Hawaii).

leg. One portion of a multisport event, for example: swim leg, bike leg, and run leg.

MOPer. Middle-of-the-pack triathlete (someone who typically finishes races in times that are considered average).

newbie. A novice triathlete.

poser. A triathlete who has all the expensive gear, but does little training.

road rash. A skin scrape caused by a bicycle accident.

RPMs. Revolutions per minute.

spinning. Pedaling at a rate of 85 to 95 revolutions per minute. This is considered a good base training technique on the bike and helps to develop an efficient pedal stroke. See cadence and RPMs.

split. A measure of time for a certain distance. Splits can refer to the time it takes to run or cycle a mile, or they can refer to a leg of the triathlon or to a transition time.

T1. Swim-to-bike transition.

T2. Bike-to-run transition.

tri-bike. Bicycle specifically designed for triathlons, characterized by steep seat tube angels, 650c wheels, and a very forward position, all geared toward improving the rider's aerodynamics and efficiency.

tri-geek. Die-hard triathlete.

wheelsucker. Unscrupulous triathlete who cheats during a race by drafting on the bike.

For More Information . . .

Total Immersion Camps and Products

Terry Laughlin puts on his Total Immersion swim camps all around the country, but he also offers a video and workbook package to learn his swimming techniques on your own, which he calls a "Self-Improvement Seminar." Call the following number for the latest pricing and to place your order, or visit Total Immersion Online (see the Internet section).

Total Immersion
Phone: 800-609-7946
E-mail: info@totalimmersion.net

Troy Jacobson's Personal Coaching

Professional triathlete and coach Troy Jacobson offers personal coaching services, as well as various training videos to triathletes at all levels of experience. Call the following number or send e-mail to contact Troy or to place your order. Also, see his Web page (see the Internet section).

Troy Jacobson's Personal Coaching
Phone: 410-583-8957
E-mail: trnrt@aol.com

National Organizations

The following national organizations specialize in some of the sports discussed throughout the book. A national organization can help you to familiarize yourself with other athletes, coaches, and events in your area.

Triathlon

USA Triathlon; P.O. Box 15820; Colorado Springs, CO; 80935-5820; Ph. 719-597-9090

TRI-CANADA; 1154 W. 24th St.; N. Vancouver, BC V6V2J2; Ph. 604-987-0092

Swimming

United States Swimming; 1750 E. Boulder St.; Colorado Springs, CO 80909; Ph. 719-578-4578

United States Masters Swimming; 2 Peter Ave.; Rutland, MA 01543; Ph. 508-886-6631

Cycling

United States Cycling Federation; 1750 E. Boulder St.; Colorado Springs, CO 80909; Ph. 719-578-4581

League of American Wheelmen; 190 W. Ostend St., Ste. 120; Baltimore, MD 21230-3755; Ph. 301-944-3399

Rails to Trails Conservancy; 913 W. Holmes, #145; Lansing, MI 48910; Ph. 517-393-6022

Women's Cycling Network; P.O. Box 303; Lansing, MI 48910; Ph. 414-736-2453

Running

USA Track & Field; P.O. Box 120; Indianapolis, IN 46206; Ph. 317-261-0500

American Running & Fitness Association; 4405 East West Highway #405; Bethesda, MD 20814; Ph. 301-913-9517

Road Runners Club of America; 629 S. Washington St.; Alexand0ria, VA 22314; Ph. 703-836-0558

Race Information

Race information is routinely published in the periodicals for each sport and on the Internet. The Danskin Race Series is for women only and does a nice job of catering to the needs of the newcomer to the sport:

Danskin Race Series; 111 W. 40th, 18th Floor; New York, NY 10018; Ph. 800-452-9526

Periodicals

Bicycle Guide; P.O. Box 55729; Boulder, CO 80322; Ph. 800-456-6501

Bicycling; 33 E. Minor St.; Emmaus, PA 18098; Ph. 800-441-7761

Inside Triathlon; 1830 N. 55th St.; Boulder, CO 80301; Ph. 800-825-8793

Runner's World; 33 E. Minor St.; Emmaus, PA 18098

Running Times; 251 Danbury Rd.; Wilton, CT 06897; Ph. 800-877-5402

Swim Magazine; P.O. Box 91870; Pasadena, CA 91109-9769; Ph. 310-607-9956

Triathlete; 1415 Third St.; Santa Monica, CA 90401; Ph. 800-441-1666

Books

Body, Mind and Sport, John Douillard, Harmony Books, 1994.

"Carbohydrates and athletic performance," E. Coyle, *Sports Science Exchange* (1988): 7.

The Complete Book of Running, Jim Fixx, Random House, 1977.

Endurance Athlete's Edge, Mark Evans, Human Kinetics, 1997.

Endurance Training for Serious Athletes, Rob Sleamaker, Human Kinetics, 1997.

The Heart Rate Monitor Book, Sally Edwards, Polar, 1992.

Lore of Running, Tim Noakes, Leisure Press, 1991.

Nancy Clark's Sports Nutrition Guidebook, Nancy Clark, Leisure Press, 1990.

Nutrition for Women, the Complete Guide, Elizabeth Somer, Henry Holt & Company, 1993.

Peak Fitness for Women, Paula Newby-Fraser with John M. Mora, Human Kinetics, 1995.

The Seven Habits of Highly Effective People, Stephen R. Lovey, New York: Simon & Schuster.

Swim, Bike, Run, Glenn Town, Human Kinetics, 1994.

Time-Saving Training for Multi-Sport Athletes, Rick Niles, Human Kinetics, 1997.

Triathlons for Fun, S. Edwards, Triathlete Magazine, 1992.

Internet

The Internet is a great resource for beginning triathletes with several sites that can answer your questions and provide opportunities to compare training notes. Check out the Usenet rec.sports newsgroup, where newcomers and professionals alike exchange news and viewpoints. The Internet also makes it easy to subscribe to any triathlon publication and join USA Triathlon. With the help of a search engine (such as Yahoo), you can also find plenty of information on swimming, cycling, and running. Of course, things are constantly changing on the Internet, so don't be surprised if some of these Web site addresses have changed:

Inside Triathlon Interactive
http://www.insidetri.com/

The Triathlete's Web
http://w3.one.net/~triweb/triweb.html

Total Immersion Swimming
http://www.totalimmersion.net

Troy Jacobson's Personal Coaching
http://coachtroy.com

Triathlete Magazine Online
http://www.triathletemag.com/

USA Triathlon Home Page
http://www.usatriathlon.org/

Bibliography

Covey, S.R. (1989). *The seven habits of highly effective people.* New York: Simon & Schuster.

Coyle, E. (1988). Carbohydrates and athletic performance. *Sports Science Exchange*, 7.

Douillard, J. (1994). *Body, mind and sport.* New York: Harmony Books.

Edwards, S. (1992). *Triathlons for fun.* Santa Monica, CA: Triathlete Magazine.

Fixx, J. (1977). *The complete book of running.* New York: Random House.

Galloway, J. (1984). *Galloway's book on running.* Bolinas, CA: Shelter Publications.

Hubbarb, R.W., Sandick, B.L., Mathew, W.T., Francesconi, R.P., Sampson, J.B., Dorkot, M.J., Maller, O., & Engell, D.B. (1984). Voluntary dehyration and alliesthesia for water. *Journal of Applied Physiology*, 868-875.

Ivy, J.L., Katz, A.L., Cutler, C.L., Sherman, W.M., & Coyle, E.F. (1988). Muscle glycogen synthesis after execise: effect of time of carbohydrate ingestion. *Journal of Applied Physiology*, 1480.

Laughlin, T. (1997). *The guide to fishlike swimming* (self-published).

Mangi, R., Jokl, P. & Dayton, O.W. (1979). *The runner's complete medical guide.* New York: Summit Books.

Mann, M. (1992). Static active stretching training for a healthy back. *The Spine Surgeon.*

Mora, J.M. (1993, April). Tapering tips. *Running Times*, 19.

Newby-Fraser, P. (1995). *Peak fitness for women.* Champaign, IL: Human Kinetics.

Plant, M. (1987). *Iron will.* Chicago: Contemporary Books.

Sheehand, G. (1989). *Personal best.* Emmaus, PA: Rodale Press.

Sherman, W.M. (1989). Pre-event nutrition. *Sports Science Exhchange.*

Sherman, W.M. (1989). Effects of 4 h pre-exercise carbohydrate feedings on cycling performance. *Medicine and Science in Sports and Exercise*, 598.

Sherman, W.M. (1991). Carbohydrate feedings 1 h before exercise improves cycling performances. *American Journal of Clinical Nutrition*, 866.

Sleamaker, R. (1997). *Endurance training for serious athletes.* Champaign, IL: Leisure Press.

Sullivan, M.E. (1993, January). Stretch—it feels good. *Current Health*, 4.

Work, J.A. (1991, January). Are java junkies poor sports? *The Physician and Sports Medicine*, 83-88.

Zawadzki, K.M., Yaspelskis, B.B., III, & Ivy, J.L. (1992). Carbohydrate-protein complex increases the rate of muscle glycogen storage after

Index

About the Author

John M. Mora is a nationally renowned sports, health and fitness, and medical writer. He is a former contributing editor to *Triathlete* and is the running columnist and triathlon feature writer for *Windy City Sports.* He has published over 300 articles, having appeared in such national magazines as *American Health, Women's Sports & Fitness,* and *Runner's World.* He is also owner of Creative CopyWriting, a copywriting business specializing in writing brochures and direct mail copy for companies in the health and fitness industry. Born in Chicago, Mora has competed around the country in 10 marathons, 70 running and cycling events, and 60 triathlons of various distances, from sprint to Ironman. He lives and trains in Plainfield, Illinois, a southwest suburb of Chicago.

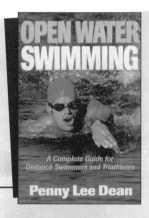